PRAIS
THE JAPAN
UNDERSTANDING
JAPANESE CULTURE,
EDITED BY ROGER J. DAVIES AND OSAMU IKENO

### "Bursting with powerful analysis"
The Daily Yomiuri, September 8, 2002

- The best introduction to Japanese society since Takie and William Lebra's landmark 1970s reader *Japanese Culture and Behavior.*
- The text is a model of plain, clear English.
- A book stuffed to bursting with powerful analysis and sparkling intuition.

### "Required reading"
The Times of London, January 15, 2004

- Cited in *The Times of London* as required reading for individuals wanting to learn more about contemporary Japanese culture.

### "A marvelous book"
Shinichi Yamanaka: Director, General Affairs Division
Japanese Ministry of Education *(Monbukagakusho)*

- *The Japanese Mind* will benefit many foreign students who want to study about Japan and will also help many Japanese students who would like to explain key concepts of Japanese culture.
- I hope this book will help to span East and West.

### "Immensely enlightening"
Robert O'Neill: Author and EFL textbook writer

- Clearly written, extremely informative, and very useful.
- Helps enormously in understanding what is going on in the minds of Japanese students.
- A good and useful book—a classic.

### "Thought provoking"
Emeritus Professor Carl James
Chairman: The Association of Language Awareness

- A highly commendable book that should appeal to a wide readership.

### "Outstanding writing"
Susan Keith, International Culture Major, Boise State University
Letter to Tuttle Publications

- As a student, I sincerely applaud this book—it is honest, dedicated, experienced, and supremely understandable.
- My highest compliments to the authors—I have never been so intellectually enlightened and informed."

ROGER J. DAVIES

# JAPANESE CULTURE

The Religious and Philosophical Foundations

**TUTTLE** Publishing

Tokyo | Rutland, Vermont | Singapore

## "Books to Span the East and West"

Tuttle Publishing was founded in 1832 in the small New England town of Rutland, Vermont [USA]. Our core values remain as strong today as they were then—to publish best-in-class books which bring people together one page at a time. In 1948, we established a publishing outpost in Japan—and Tuttle is now a leader in publishing English-language books about the arts, languages and cultures of Asia. The world has become a much smaller place today and Asia's economic and cultural influence has grown. Yet the need for meaningful dialogue and information about this diverse region has never been greater. Over the past seven decades, Tuttle has published thousands of books on subjects ranging from martial arts and paper crafts to language learning and literature—and our talented authors, illustrators, designers and photographers have won many prestigious awards. We welcome you to explore the wealth of information available on Asia at www.tuttlepublishing.com.

Published by Tuttle Publishing, an imprint of Periplus Editions (HK) Ltd.

www.tuttlepublishing.com

Text & Photos Copyright © 2016
Roger J. Davies

ISBN 978-4-8053-1163-9

26 25 24 23    5 4 3 2

Printed in Malaysia    2312VP

TUTTLE PUBLISHING® is a registered trademark of Tuttle Publishing, a division of Periplus Editions (HK) Ltd.

**Distributed by**

**North America, Latin America & Europe**
Tuttle Publishing
364 Innovation Drive
North Clarendon
VT 05759-9436 U.S.A.
Tel: (802) 773-8930
Fax: (802) 773-6993
info@tuttlepublishing.com
www.tuttlepublishing.com

**Japan**
Tuttle Publishing
Yaekari Building, 3rd Floor
5-4-12 Osaki, Shinagawa-ku
Tokyo 141 0032
Tel: (81) 3 5437-0171
Fax: (81) 3 5437-0755
sales@tuttle.co.jp
www.tuttle.co.jp

**Asia Pacific**
Berkeley Books Pte. Ltd.
3 Kallang Sector #04-01
Singapore 349278
Tel: (65) 6741-2178
Fax: (65) 6741-2179
inquiries@periplus.com.sg
www.tuttlepublishing.com

# CONTENTS

# PREFACE

The genesis of *Japanese Culture: The Religious and Philosophical Foundations* evolved out of many years of classroom instruction designed for international business students in an MBA program at Hitotsubashi University in Tokyo, Japan. The lectures, entitled "A Brief Journey Through Japanese Cultural History," attempted to guide the students through the multiple layers of religious and philosphical belief that underlie life in modern-day Japan. Topics included the importance of such historical elements in the development of the Japanese aesthetic and martial arts, the Japanese style of learning, and the traditional values of contemporary Japanese people. The goal was to paint a picture of Japanese culture in "broad strokes" so that participants could better understand the historical complexities of what they were seeing during their stay in Japan. These lectures were then further field tested with both undergraduate and postgraduate Japanese students studying English at an advanced level at The University of Tokyo and Waseda University (earlier unfinished drafts had also been developed at Ehime University in Matsuyama, Japan). The result of all of these efforts is the present volume.

*Japanese Culture: The Religious and Philosophical Foundations* begins with two introductory chapters, one investigating the origins of the Japanese, and the other exploring the most important approaches to Japanese cultural history found in current scholarship. A conceptual framework developed by cultural anthropologists to explain Japan's diverse religious and philosophical traditions, known as the multilayered model, is then introduced. Subsequent chapters examine each of these layers in a timeline stretching from Japan's ancient past to modern times in the following sequence:

Shinto, Buddhism, Taoism, Zen, Confucianism, and Western influences of the modern era.

Each chapter in this volume concludes with extensive endnotes and thought-provoking discussion activities, many of which were created by the students with whom this book was field tested. The chapters are also twinned with illustrated appendices, which provide perspective and depth to the selected themes. A detailed bibliography is included for readers who wish to further explore the book's topics.

Finally, the author wishes to express his thanks and gratitude to the hundreds of students, both Japanese and non-Japanese, who participated in this project over many years. This book is dedicated to you.

Roger J. Davies, PhD, MBA
Tokyo, Japan

# JAPANESE CHRONOLOGY

**Note**: There continue to be disagreements concerning the exact dates of the periods listed below. However, the following timeline seems to be widely accepted.

### ANCIENT (Kodai)

| | |
|---|---|
| Jōmon Period | 8,000–300 BC |
| Yayoi Period | 300 BC–250 AD |
| Kofun [Tomb] Period | 250–646 AD |
| Nara Period | 646–794 AD |
| Heian Period | 794–1185 AD |

### MEDIEVAL (Chūsei)

| | |
|---|---|
| Kamakura Period | 1185–1392 AD |
| Nanbokuchō Period | 1336–1392 AD |
| Muromachi Period | 1392–1603 AD |

### EARLY MODERN (Kinsei)

| | |
|---|---|
| Edo Period (Tokugawa Shogunate) | 1603–1868 AD |

### MODERN (Kin-Gendai)

| | |
|---|---|
| Meiji Period | 1868–1912 AD |
| Taishō Period | 1912–1926 AD |
| Shōwa Period | 1926–1989 AD |
| Heisei Period | 1989–present |

# JAPANESE
# CULTURE

# The Origins of the Japanese

The origins of the Japanese people and their culture date back to a time of remote antiquity of which we have almost no knowledge. As a result, there are still many unanswered questions and numerous areas of dispute and contention. Evidence of the origins of the Japanese comes from three main sources: archeological remains, written Han Chinese documents and early Japanese records,[1] and as the results of studies in comparative linguistics[2] (Sansom, 1976; Reischauer, 1988).

No traces of paleolithic (early Stone Age) culture have been distinguished in Japan, but two types of neolithic (late Stone Age) culture have been identified: Jōmon (named after a characteristic "rope-pattern" type of pottery) and Yayoi (named for a kind of pottery found at a place of that name). Technically, Jōmon pottery is considered to be inferior to Yayoi, but artistically, it is more advanced (Sansom, 1976, p. 2). Both kinds of pottery have been discovered throughout the Japanese archipelago, but the Jōmon type is more predominant in the north and east while Yayoi pottery is found more extensively in the south and west. The culture of the

Jōmon pottery

Jōmon Clay Figurine

Jōmon Architecture

Yayoi period (300 BC–250 AD) is thus thought to have originated in Kyushu between the third and second centuries
BC, and is characterized by the wet cultivation of rice and
the introduction of metals such as bronze and iron. The
neolithic culture of Japan is felt to have reached high levels
of development and it is, therefore, thought to have been
of very long duration (ibid., p. 4). It came to an end with the
introduction of metal culture from China, but lasted until
the first century BC in the west, the second century AD in
central Japan, and in the far north until c. 1000 AD. Bronze

Yayoi Village

Age culture had reached its height in China during the Chou dynasty (1122–221 BC), and spread slowly to southern Manchuria, Korea, and then to Japan; with the Han dynasty (202 BC–220 AD) China entered the Iron Age. No sooner did the Bronze Age begin in Japan, however, than it was eclipsed by the Iron Age culture of a rapidly expanding Han civilization from China.[3] As a result, Japan is said to have had no true Bronze Age culture of its own.

Japan is thought to have endured numerous waves of migration during her long prehistory, and so "the Japanese race is a compound of elements drawn in ancient times [mainly] from different parts of the Asian mainland. The order in which these elements arrived and the proportions in which they are mixed cannot be definitely stated, [however]" (ibid., p. 1). The Japanese archipelago acted as a kind of cul-de-sac for tribes migrating through Asia, driven eastward because of hunger, fear, or perhaps the desire for change. The most predominant racial strain is considered to have been from Mongol tribes arriving through Korea. Their influence is seen in a variety of aspects of Japanese life: the earliest religion (Shinto) has much in common with the Sha-

manism of north-east Asia, weapons discovered at archeological sites resemble those of Mongolian peoples, and the
Japanese physical type is Mongoloid (i.e., Japanese people
have eyelids with a "Mongol [epicanthic] fold" and babies
are born with a characteristic "Mongol spot"). However,
there are also some features from southern China evident in
Japan, including the wet cultivation of rice and the Japanese
physique, which is more like the southern Chinese than
their northerly taller and sturdier neighbors. There are even
proto-Malay traces in the Japanese racial make-up probably
due to migrations along the *kuroshio* (the Black Current) from
Indonesia, Malaysia, and even Polynesia (Sansom, 1976, p. 6;
Reishauer, 1988, p. 34). All of these migrations displaced the
original inhabitants of the Japanese archipelago, known as
the Ainu, a Caucasoid people resembling the tribes of eastern Siberia. The Ainu have a characteristic hairiness of face
and body, accounting perhaps for the somewhat greater
hairiness of the Japanese compared with other Mongoloid
peoples, and until the eighth century AD they occupied the
northern third of Honshu (today less than 20,000 survive in
Hokkaido and they are on the brink of extinction). By the
Christian era in the West, there was, however, a fairly uniform civilization in Japan. Racial and ethnic blending and
fusion had taken place, and even though migrations continued from the Korean peninsula up until the eighth century
AD, "the Japanese developed a picture of themselves as a
racially distinct and 'pure' group, often portrayed in terms
of a single great family" (Reischauer, 1988, p. 34). From the
eighth century until the present day, however, there has
been virtually no infusion of new blood into Japan (ibid.).

The first glimpse of early Japanese life is afforded by Han
Chinese records of the 3rd century AD—the Japanese are
described as a people having sharp class distinctions, making their living by agriculture and fishing, and divided into
a hundred or more tribal units, some with women rulers

(Reischauer, 1988, p. 42). Japan was known to the Chinese of this time as the "Kingdom of Wa,"[4] as well as the "Queen's Country."[5] These Han dynasty records also describe the early Japanese as follows:

> They take their food with their hands, but have wooden trays . . . to place it on. They are a long-lived race, and persons who have reached 100 are very common. All men of high rank have four or five wives; others two or three. There is no robbery or theft, and litigation is infrequent. The men, both small and great, tatoo their faces and work designs on their bodies. They have distinctions of rank, and some are vassals of others. (Sansom, 1976, pp. 29–30)

Han historians also recorded with admiration the gentleness and loyalty of Japanese women, that theft was almost unknown, and that the laws and social customs of the Japanese were very strict (ibid., p. 52). It is clear, however, that indigenous Japanese culture was not at a very high level at this time. There was a scanty population in small groups of dwelling houses along the coasts or on the banks of streams. Rice was cultivated and rice wine was made from very early times. Fishing and hunting were important, and the population was settled in numerous, small agricultural communities. Garments were primitive, although there was free use of jewelry and semi-precious stones (ibid., p. 45).

Starting in the 3rd century AD, it is thought that Japan was overrun by waves of mounted invaders from the Korean peninsula, and during the next three centuries large burial mounds were built suggesting concentrations of wealth and power in the hands of a military upper class (Reischauer, 1988, p. 42). These sepulchral mounds were of enormous size and were composed of great piles of earth over a stone burial chamber. These tombs were found chiefly in west-

Kofun Burial Mound

ern and central Japan and contained metal weapons, armor, helmets, and horse-trappings (Sansom, 1976, p. 12). This period, called the Kofun (Tomb) era (250–646 AD), marks the beginning of state formation in Japan.

By the end of the first century AD, some clans in Kyushu, making use of superior weapons and equipment derived from Korea and China, began to push eastward and assert their authority. They slowly proceeded along the Inland Sea until they reached the Yamato (Nara) plain, where they established a central state. By the sixth century AD, this central state had gained some control over western and central Japan, perhaps as far north as Sendai. At this time, the political and economic organization of the region was still relatively undeveloped, with semiautonomous tribal units owning the land and pledging allegiance to the central clan at Yamato (Sansom, 1976, p. 24).

Virtually all cultural influences on the early Japanese derived directly or indirectly from continental China, which at a time when Japanese life was still rudimentary, possessed perhaps the most highly developed civilization in the known world. Because of Japan's geographical placement on the outer extremity of the Pacific Rim, civilization was a comparatively late development in the region. As Sansom (1976, p. 39) notes, "in studying early Japanese society, one is impressed by its [isolation and] late development. We are accustomed to think of the history of Asian cultures as reaching far back into an enlightened antiquity; but this is by no means true of Japan." Reischauer (1988, p. 41) concurs: "The [Japanese] islands were thousands of years behind Europe, the Middle East, the Indian subcontinent, and China in the introduction of agriculture and centuries behind in the use of bronze and iron." It is thought that these metals, as well as more advanced agricultural techniques, entered Japan at the same time in the third and second centuries BC, due to contact with China. Japan's political relations with the mainland also commenced at a very early date, not later than the first century BC (Sansom, 1976, p. 41).[6] Japan even maintained a foothold on the Korean peninsula during the first centuries AD and was continually involved in political intrigues among the kingdoms there. There was also frequent intermarriage between the ruling houses of Japan and Korea. Chinese writing was officially adopted at the beginning of the fifth century AD, which was a landmark in Japanese history as it "shaped the subsequent development of nearly every Japanese institution," but it is a mistake to assume, as is sometimes done, that the influence of China was of no great importance up until this time. In fact, Chinese influence was a persistent, increasing, and overwhelming factor of early Japanese life starting from the first century BC (ibid., p. 44).

NOTES

1. The two official Japanese records which are sources of information, the *Kojiki* ("Record of Ancient Things") and *Nihongi* (or more correctly, *Nihon-shoki*: "Chronicles of Japan"), written in 712 AD and 720 AD respectively, are considered to be somewhat tendentious works in which myth and legend and history were combined to enhance the prestige of the ruling dynasty, and should be viewed with caution (Sansom, 1976, p. 20).

2. Comparative linguistics has analyzed Japanese in relation to a variety of other languages in an attempt to shed light on its origins. Japanese is classified as belonging to the Ural-Altaic language family along with such languages as Finnish, Turkish, Mongolian, and the dialects spoken by the Tungusic tribes of eastern Siberia (Miller, 1982).

3. Han culture at this time was like "a gigantic explosion of energies slowly stored up since the dawn of Chinese civilization." It thrust out and expanded throughout Asia in all directions (Sansom, 1976, p. 17).

4. Because the character "*wa*" had the meaning of dwarf, this could have been a kind of epithet frequently used by the Chinese in relation to other peoples, or the Japanese may indeed have been short in stature.

5. This perhaps indicates a matriarchal lineage in early Japanese culture.

6. Thus, as Sansom (1976, p. 41) points out, Japan's isolation is a relatively late phenomenon in her history.

## DISCUSSION ACTIVITIES

1. Discuss the teaching of history in Japanese schools, what students are taught, and how they are taught it. In your opinion, what can be done to improve the teaching of history so that Japanese young people can have a better understanding of their own culture?

2. It is said that the Japanese are a homogeneous people, often likened to one large tribe. Discuss this point of view from the perspective of your reading on the origins of the Japanese.

3. Why is it so difficult to obtain reliable information about the origins of the Japanese?

4. In what ways are modern Japanese similar to, or different from, the descriptions provided by Han Chinese records of the 3rd century AD?

5. Discuss the influence of China and Korea on the development of Japanese culture from its origins to the present day.

6. In 2001, a 65 million yen research project entitled "An Interdisciplinary Study of the Origins of the Japanese Peoples and Cultures," was carried out with government cooperation, culminating in an NHK documentary and book series called, "The Japanese: The Long Journey" (see Appendix A). In this investigation, researchers conducted a study of the facial features of 1,047 randomly selected Japanese. Of them, 35.1% were found to fit the northern Asian type, commonly found in the people of northern China; 22% were categorized as Korean Peninsula; 28.3%, southern China; 13.3% Indochina; and 5.1% fitted the facial features typi-

cal of the southern Pacific region. Genetic and archaeological analysis indicates that Japan has been a grand melting pot of peoples who came here from Siberia via the Ice Age landbridge through Sakhalin; from northern and southern Asia via the Korean Peninsula; and by boat from Indochina and Polynesia via the Ryukyu archipelago. The high percentage of "northern Asian" faces is mostly a legacy of the large-scale immigration from the mainland through Korea, and the subsequent population explosion that began some 2,300 years ago in the early Yayoi Period. Discuss the multiethnic origins of the Japanese from the perspective of this NHK study.

# Approaches to Japanese Cultural History

## INTRODUCTION

A number of conceptual models[1] have been developed by
scholars in order to explain the evolution of world civilizations. Perhaps the best known was put forward by the twentieth century historian, Arnold Toynbee, who applied the
analogy of the living organism to the study of culture, suggesting that all civilizations go through a cycle of birth, life,
and decay:

> At the time of its birth each civilization . . . is faced with
> its own particular challenges. If the challenges are met
> and overcome, the civilization grows; if the responses
> are inadequate, the civilization dies. Response is deter-
> mined by the inner energy and spirit of the civilization.
> Once established, a civilization appears to pass through
> certain stages of development: a time of growth . . .; a
> time of troubles; and then an attempted resurgence. . . .
> Thereafter the civilization declines. But it has been
> possible for old civilizations to give birth to new ones

through the revitalizing spiritual force of new and more
universal spiritual beliefs. (Hall & Beardsley, 1965, p. 125)

In East Asia, Toynbee concludes that there have been two
major civilizations, both of which were centered in China.
The first spanned almost two millennia, beginning in the
Shang dynasty (c. 1500 BC) and reaching its height during the Han dynasty (202 BC–220 AD); the second occurred
during the Sui and T'ang dynasties (589–907 AD) due to the
spiritual force of Buddhism. He treats Japan as an offshoot
of these civilizations, but with a semi-autonomous character because of the great challenge presented by the sea gap
between Japan and the Asian continent. Toynbee's ideas
have never been applied to a full-scale history of Japan, but
his model continues to have advocates among contemporary historians.

Karl Jaspers, the German philosopher and historian,
provided another approach to the development of world
civilization in which history itself is seen as a process of
continuous growth encompassing clearly defined stages
(ibid., p. 126):

(1)  the primitive state: man existed in isolated social
pockets

(2)  the early regional civilizations, such as Greece, Egypt,
and China

(3)  the great cultures that developed through the unifying ideas of universal religions

(4)  "one world" (yet to be achieved) through the spread
of science

Jaspers was particularly fascinated by one period of human history, from the seventh to the fourth centuries BC, known as the Axial Age, when a number of great historical figures arose at approximately the same time in different cultures: Confucius and Lao-tzu in China, Gautama Buddha in India, Zarathustra in Persia, the prophets in Israel, and the philosophers in Greece (see Appendix B). At this time in world history, "man first became conscious of himself and his cosmic limitations [and] he experimented with and developed the categories of thought and reasoning that are still used today" (ibid.). For Jaspers, Japan remained in an undeveloped, prehistorical condition until it was brought under Chinese influence, at which time it entered the stream of world events.

The views of historians such as Toynbee and Jaspers have in common a belief that human society, whether East or West, can be explained by a uniform theory of development, regardless of the widely differing conceptions of what the essential moving forces of history might be. However, many writers have also insisted on the existence of certain fundamental differences between Eastern and Western ways of thinking. Typical of this approach is F.S.C. Northrop, who sees East and West as deeply divided by contrasting philosophical and religious approaches to life: "The West uses logic, analysis, categories . . .; the East uses intuition and direct apperception . . ." (ibid., pp. 127–128). Northrop places Japan among the nations of the East with its common heritage in Confucianism, Taoism, and Buddhism, but draws a distinction between Japan and other Eastern nations because of the speed with which the country was able to industrialize after 1868, suggesting that modern Japan is a meeting place, or bridge, between East and West.

For those who wish to understand the complexities and contradictions of modern Japan, history is of primary importance. The present is mirrored in the past, and the past exists in the present in the unconscious cultural heritage of a people, in the structure of their social and political institutions, and in the value systems they have created. During the course of its long history, Japanese culture has appeared in a number of different manifestations, each characterized by certain distinct behavioral patterns and sets of belief. Each of these phases of historical development has contributed to the cumulative growth of Japanese culture and has given rise to traditions which continue to play an important role in contemporary Japanese life. However, "history as remembered or recorded is inevitably a selection out of the infinitude of the past" (ibid., p. 122), and history as it happened and history as it is written are not always the same. The cultural history of Japan, in particular, has been "set down in many different styles and from many different points of view," and the wide variety of interpretations stem from underlying assumptions that need to be carefully examined. Such assumptions may be crude or sophisticated, they may be honest and objective or they may arise from certain ideologies or conscious biases. "They are not equally valid" (ibid., p. 123).

## GEOGRAPHICAL DETERMINISM

One conceptual model for understanding Japanese cultural history is known as geographical (or environmental) determinism. In this way of thinking, there is said to be a direct relationship between a people's natural and social environment and their patterns of life. In fact, a great many observers have seized on some feature or other of Japan's natural environment as the key to understanding Japanese culture or the temperament of its people:

> The ever-present threat of earthquakes, tidal waves, typhoons, and other natural dangers is supposed to

Traditional Rice Fields

make the Japanese fatalistic, violent, or poignantly aware of nature and its precarious beauty. The ever-visible mountains or fields are said to induce serenity; or else, depending on the theorizer, the small-scale . . . villages create . . . a sensitivity to social nuances. (ibid., pp. 3–4)

Whether there is any truth to popular myths about the relationship between the geography of Japan and Japanese culture is open to debate, since the heterogeneity of the natural environment of the Japanese archipelago gives rise to a wide range of contradictory generalizations. In fact, the geographical determinism model turns out to be far too sim-plistic to serve as an effective conceptual framework for any comprehensive understanding of Japanese culture.

Bamboo Forest

## Nihonjinron

Another conceptual model which has gained both popularity and notoriety in the post-war era is known as *nihonjinron*, or "the theory of Japanese uniqueness." In essence, *nihonjinron* explains Japanese cultural history and behavior by claiming that the Japanese are somehow distinguished by special "racial characteristics."[2] The origin's of Japan's sense of uniqueness are to be found in a number of important factors, including . . .

> . . . its long history of isolation, at first natural but later self-imposed, its distinctive culture, its unusual type of language, its unique and very difficult writing system, and its strong patterns of group organization. Above the close-knit family stood the local community, above it the feudal domain or modern company, and at the top the nation, which was geographically, linguistically, and culturally very distinct from all others. To the Japanese the world seemed quite obviously divided between Japan and the rest of the world. (Reischauer, 1988, p. 395)

The "unique" features possessed by the Japanese are said to include such characteristics as an unusual understanding of nature and an innate sense of beauty. A government textbook, *Kokutai no hongi*, expresses a nationalistic version of this belief, stating that "Japan possesses a unique national structure (the idea of *kokutai*) [which involves] a marked ability to absorb foreign cultural elements, to perfect these elements beyond the state in which they were received, and then to add them to the indigenous culture without losing the essence of Japan's individuality" (ibid., pp. 150–151).

Beginning in the 1970s, but continuing up to the present day, numerous "pop culture" books and articles have also been written by Japanese intellectuals stressing the singularity of some aspect of Japan's culture. The theory of the "uniqueness" of Japanese behavior, physiology, language, and culture includes such topics as the supposed homogeneity of the Japanese people (i.e., "racially pure"), the "island nation theory" (*shima guni konjō*), and the notion that *nihongo* is a wholly unique language for which the Japanese have developed "specialized left brain / right brain functions." Many Japanese magazines still commonly carry articles on the "uniqueness" of the Japanese brain, nose, weather, geography, and so forth.

Of late, however, *nihonjinron* has come in for some sharp criticism and widespread condemnation. For example:

> Some writers have employed wild generalizations and highly questionable methodology. The crudest examples argue that the Japanese have anatomically unique brains, or that they communicate telepathically. Collectively, such books constitute an ideology with clear racist and nationalistic overtones. (LaPenta, 1998, p. 15)

Most observers feel that *nihonjinron* writing is not only rather absurd, but also dangerous. Over the years, the Japanese have produced a culture that has many distinct features, and when uniqueness does exist it should be recognized. But prejudicial and xenophobic distinctions such as those mentioned above have no place in serious scholarship, nor in rational discussions on international culture or Japan's place in the modern world. As the cultural anthropologist Emiko Ohnuki-Tierney points out, most of the Japanese features that are described as unique are not uniquely Japanese when taken separately. Like all other cultures in the world, "the uniqueness that distinguishes Japanese culture from other cultures emerges with a unique combination of factors which are not unique in themselves" (1984, p. 2). Historian Kenichi Matsumoto concurs: "What is perceived as Japanese uniqueness is fictional to a significant degree . . . yet it is deeply ingrained in the minds of the people" (Sasamoto, 1999, p. 7).

As both Ohnuki-Tierney and Matsumoto (ibid.) point out, it should be obvious that all peoples of the world have their own unique histories and cultures—the Japanese are not the only people who can hear the sounds of nature, nor is Japan the only country in the world with distinct seasons, and it is unnecessary to constantly call attention to one's unique-ness as some Japanese intellectuals do. The Japanese are different to some extent, but then so is every ethnic group in the world. More importantly, however, the *nihonjinron* model is clearly inadequate in preparing Japanese people, especially the young, for understanding the rapid changes that are taking place in their country and the world today: "At present, many Japanese . . . are unsure about who they are and where their country is heading, although they may enjoy affluent lives. Politicians have failed to offer any ideas. But it seems to me that the Japanese have to answer these questions in this globalized world" (Matsumoto; as cited in Sasamoto, ibid.).

## THE MULTILAYERED MODEL

In short, the two models outlined above both fall short in viewing Japanese national traits as being inborn and immu-table, and fail to distinguish between individual and group characteristics. A third conceptual framework which avoids these shortcomings and which is far more useful in under-standing Japanese cultural history is sometimes termed *the multilayered model*. In this way of thinking, Japanese culture is conceived as a structure composed of successive layers, in which new strata are superimposed upon the old. The layers themselves are thought to be the main formative elements of Japanese religious and philosophical thought—Shinto, Buddhism, Taoism, and Confucianism—on top of which is overlaid the secular and technological influences of Western culture in modern times (see Appendix C).[3]

There is, however, a long history of scholarly debate about the nature of the religious and philosophical beliefs of the Japanese, especially in light of the fact that many people subscribe to more than one religion: "[T]he current controversy among scholars of Japanese culture [lies] over whether or not various religions (Buddhism, Shintoism, Taoism, and folk religions) constitute a multilayered structure or a single fused structure" (Ohnuki-Tierney, 1984, p. 9). Organizationally and ideologically, a number of religions have co-existed since ancient times, and they still remain separate and distinct systems. On the other hand, when viewed from the participation of the individual, a merger or combination of religious beliefs seems to occur. Two crucial points must be kept in mind in this controversy. First, there is a distinction in perspectives—whether one looks at these Japanese religions in terms of their institutional-organizational frameworks and their orthodox doctrinal practices, or in terms of the way people view and practice them. The second problem is related to lay perception, or whether these religions are seen and practiced as one cultural system, or as separate systems used in combination, by ordinary Japanese citizens. Most Japanese are at least nominally both Buddhist and Shintoist at the same time, but no one, no matter how indifferent they are toward religions, would confuse a buddha with a *kami* (i.e., a Shinto "god").

Resolution of this issue is not our goal. In terms of the meaning and functions assigned to religions by ordinary people, "the scale tips towards the 'fused' end" (ibid., p. 149), but in terms of understanding and analysis, the "multilayered" perspective is more useful. In particular, for those trying to grasp Japanese cultural history, this multilayered model allows for the separation of a complex blend of difficult issues into distinct elements for examination and discussion.

This will also lead to clear and logical explanations of many of the contradictions inherent in modern Japanese life.[4]

## THE FOUNDATIONS OF JAPANESE CULTURE

Japan is often said to be a land of contrasts, a place where the new exists side by side with the old. Beneath Japan's high-tech, modern veneer, an ageless core lives on, or as Ohnuki-Tierney (1984, p. 71) states, "industrialized and otherwise modernized Japan continues to exhibit many features characteristic of primitive worlds." Perhaps more than in any other country today, Japan exemplifies "change within continuity" (Richie, 1995, p. 9). Matsumoto (op. cit., p. 7) describes this as follows:

> What fascinates me about Japan is the diversity and multilayered aspects of its culture, as Tenshin Okakura (1862–1913) said: "Japan is the museum of Asia." Japanese culture does not end with the tea ceremony, flower arranging or poetry. It is the product of a diverse ethnic and cultural amalgam.

Contemporary Japanese religious and philosophical thought can be characterized as multilayered, eclectic, and syncretic (i.e., discrete and often contradictory elements are often juxtaposed or harmonized without critical examination or logical unity). In Japan such diverse elements as animistic Shinto, Confucian ethics, religious Taoism, Buddhist sects, Christian denominations, and a variety of new religious cults exist side by side in relative harmony and without apparent contradiction—no one religious or philosophical tradition is dominant and each is affected by the others. The Japanese have long-held customs of plural belonging and commonly follow more than one belief system.[5]

The essence of contemporary Japanese religious and philosophical thought results from the interaction of two main
kinds of belief system: a set of indigenous, animistic practices that originated with Shinto, and the great East Asian
traditions introduced from outside Japan—Taoism, Buddhism, and Confucianism (though Taoism has had a more
indirect effect through its impact on Zen). To this may be
added the more recent influences of Western culture, which
underlie many of the technological and scientific advances
of Japan in the 20th century. Shinto, Buddhism, Taoism,
Confucianism, and modern Western influences can thus
be viewed as formative elements in the Japanese religious
and philosophical belief system, constituting a dynamic and
multilayered complex in which newer traditions are superimposed on older ones and the whole blended and modified
to fit native Japanese tastes, preferences, and attitudes.[6]

## NOTES

1. According to Enkvist (1987, pp. 27–28), a model is a simplified representation of reality. It is simplified because
it aims at reproducing a selection of relevant elements of
reality rather than all of reality at once. A theory, on the
other hand, is a set of principles on which the model is built
(though in actual practice, the two terms are sometimes
used interchangeably).

2. Nation, language, race, and culture are distinct categories for most people, but according to Reischauer (1988, p.
398), for the Japanese they are almost synonymous. Race, in
particular, plays a large part in the self-image of the Japanese, who pride themselves on their "racial purity," despite
the obvious mixture that settled the Japanese archipelago
(ibid.). Because they have merged their feelings about race,
culture, and nation together, the sense of racial difference

runs deep, and as a result, racial prejudice is a particular problem in modern Japan. It is very difficult for non-Japanese living in Japan to cross over the imaginary "racial line" and actual "culture line" into full membership in Japanese society (ibid., p. 399). The Japanese generally regard foreigners of any type as irrevocably on the other side of the dividing line between "us and them" (ibid.).

3. To study East Asian cultural history, "one must be prepared to study religions, for the Far East, especially Japan, never produced a strong branch of rationalist and secular philosophy such as flourished in the Occidental world from Greco-Roman times on" (Hall & Beardsley, 1965, p. 310). In addition, most Japanese follow more than one religion at once and place equal value on religions that are vastly different in terms of their philosophical elaboration. Moreover, the Japanese "do not particularly look on any of these religions as a main source of ethics" (ibid.):

> Shintoism, Buddhism, Confucianism, and shamanism and various other folk religions have been the religions of Japan. Shintoism, the only religion of indigenous origin, and Buddhism have traditionally been regarded as the most important. It has often been pointed out that these religions have permeated the daily lives of the Japanese; they have become part of their customs without requiring any psychological commitment on the part of the individual. Most Japanese subscribe to more than one religion, often without consciously realizing it. (Ohnuki-Tierney, 1984, p. 145)

4. It should also be noted that one of the most vexing problems in understanding Japanese culture is to determine from which particular layer certain religious practices are derived (Sansom, 1976, p. ix). Perhaps the most contentious

of these issues involves the custom of ancestor worship.
Most mainstream scholars maintain that ancestor worship
was an importation from China:

> During the most vigorous period of the T'ang Dynasty,
> the impact of Chinese civilization upon Japan reached
> such a climax that it marks the turning point in the evo-
> lution of Japanese institutions. . . . China under the early
> T'ang rulers was one of the most highly civilized states
> in the world, as well as the most powerful, and in the Far
> East had no rivals for such a distinction. Throughout the
> seventh and eighth centuries the government in Yam-
> ato sent a succession of official embassies to the T'ang
> court [and] the result was a wholesale copying of Chi-
> nese techniques and ideas affecting almost every aspect
> of Japanese life and society. . . . The Chinese classics,
> especially the Confucian writings, were studied intently,
> since every well-bred person was expected to be familiar
> with them. . . . A new emphasis was placed upon family
> solidarity and filial devotion, including the duty of sac-
> rificing to *ancestral spirits* [italics added]. (Burns & Ralph,
> 1964, p. 337)

On the other hand, as Burns and Ralph (ibid.) note, "[s]ome
Japanese scholars deny that the custom of ancestor worship
was an importation; but in any case it was intensified by
contacts with the Chinese."

5. For example, many Japanese homes contain both a miniature Shinto shrine and a Buddhist altar in their inner sanc-
tums, and (Shintoist) ancestral mortuary tablets are placed
beside the Buddhist altar during memorial observances.
Most Japanese also choose Shinto ceremonies for their wed-
dings, while Buddhist rites are reserved for funerals.

6. Only Shinto and some of the "New Religions" are indigenous to Japan; "the others have wider communities, and their origin, as well as their center of gravity is outside the country. Because of the prominence of religions of foreign origin and certain admixtures of doctrine and practice at the national level, the Japanese attitude toward religion is often described as eclectic and syncretic" (Hall & Beardsley, 1965, p. 312). However, these are highly complex issues and much depends on one's viewpoint. Religions that have co-existed for centuries in Japan remain separate and distinct systems organizationally and ideologically (e.g., Shinto and Buddhism), but in the way ordinary people practice them, they exist as a single, "fused" cultural system. Furthermore, whatever religions have been imported from abroad have certainly been "reworked to suit the Japanese cultural context rather than remaining foreign bodies attached to Japanese life" (ibid., p. 313).

## DISCUSSION ACTIVITIES

1. Do you agree with Northrop's argument that modern Japan is "a bridge between East and West?"

2. Why is Japan's cultural history so complex and difficult to understand?

3. What do you think of the viewpoint expressed in *Kokutai no hongi* that Japan has a "unique national structure?" Do you agree with the opinions of Ohnuki-Tierney and Matsumoto that "it is unnecessary to constantly call attention to Japan's uniqueness as some Japanese intellectuals do?" Why, or why not?

4. Discuss the problem of racial prejudice and discrimination in modern Japan.

5. Comment on the statement by Matsumoto that "Japanese culture does not end with the tea ceremony, flower arranging or poetry. It is the product of a diverse ethnic and cultural amalgam."

6. Discuss the role of ancestor worship in modern Japan. In your opinion, what are the origins of ancestor worship in Japanese culture?

7. Comment on the viewpoint that contemporary Japanese religious and philosophical thought can be characterized as "multilayered, eclectic, and syncretic."

# Shinto

## INTRODUCTION

Prince Shotoku,[1] the first Japanese envoy to China during the Sui Dynasty and the man credited with introducing Buddhism to Japan, coined the following famous analogy to describe Japanese religious practices (see Appendix D):

- Shinto: the roots of a tree; imbedded in the very heart of the Japanese people

- Confucianism: the trunk and branches; politics, morality, and education

- Buddhism: the flowers; religious feelings bloom as flowers

Shinto thus forms the bedrock layer of the multilayered, syncretic religious and philosophical belief system of Japan. Its origins are obscure and lie in the nation's prehistory— when the Japanese first became aware of themselves as a people, it was already there. The term Shinto ("The Way of the Gods") was coined at a later stage in Japanese history in order to distinguish the wide range of animistic practices[2] and numerous local cults native to Japan from the newly adopted Buddhist religion (c. 6th century AD).

Characteristic of all forms of Animism is their attribution of conscious life to nature or natural objects, and a belief in the existence of innumerable spirits which are thought to inhabit sacred places and which are intimately involved in human affairs. These nature spirits are thought to sanction human beings for neglect of ritual or breaking taboos, but not usually with regard to moral codes. Ceremonies are important, not in the sense of communicating with a divine creator, nor in terms of metaphysics or even how to lead a moral or ethical life, but are mostly concerned with the practicalities of daily life: securing food, curing illness, averting danger, obtaining profit, etc. The intervention of the spirit world is typically achieved through ceremonial offerings and ritual prayers.

## IMPORTANT CONCEPTS

Shinto comprises a set of animistic religious practices based on the worship of *kami* (spirits or gods), which can be natural phenomena (e.g., the sun, mountains, trees, water, rocks, etc.), mythological beings (e.g., the Sun Goddess), human beings such as ancestors, and even ideas. To the early Japanese the visible and invisible worlds were filled with powerful influences, and people believed in a vague way that all natural objects harbored a spirit, that all perceptible objects were in some way living (Sansom, 1976, p. 25). The term *kami* simply means "superior" or "above," and at one end of its spectrum of meaning is the Sun Goddess; at the other, even mud or vermin can be *kami* (ibid., p. 47). Although these early Japanese thought of the universe as composed of myriad sentient parts, it was a rather cloudy and unformulated conception (Sansom, 1976, p. 46). They believed in

Chozubachi

a great number of *kami*, both good and evil: "The chronicles tell of [*kami*] who swarmed and buzzed like flies, and of trees and herbs and rocks and streams that could all speak" (ibid., p. 25). However, the characters of these *kami* were "confused and shadowy, their power ill-defined, and their habitation either unknown or undistinguishable from ordinary beings" (ibid., p. 47). The fact that they were rarely depicted by idols or pictures is an indication of their nebulous quality in people's minds (ibid.).

In Shinto, the line between man and nature is not sharply drawn, and among the early Japanese, "there was no word for Nature as something apart and distinct from man. . . . Man was treated as an integral part of the whole, closely associated and identified with the elements and forces of the world about him" (Sakamaki, 1967, p. 24). However, although there was a strong sense of awe and reverence before nature, there was little interest in metaphysical issues:

> Before the arrival of Buddhism from the continent in
> the sixth century A.D., there was . . . little metaphysical
> speculation in Japan. There was no body of literature, no
> school of philosophy, no intellectual stimulus to encour-
> age or maintain sustained inquiries into the invisible
> imponderables of the universe. . . . The *kami* were invoked
> in prayers of thanksgiving or of supplication for some
> measure of material blessing, such as good harvests,
> protection from natural calamities and evil spirits or
> forces, freedom from sickness, and the like. (ibid., p. 26)

Nor did Shintoist beliefs offer an explicit moral code: "Concepts of moral wrongdoing or sin were barely [acknowl-
edged], so that prayers were not for forgiveness of sins or
spiritual blessedness, but for physical well-being and temporal prosperity" (ibid.). Most of the observances of Shinto
had to do with growth and decay. As a result, on the one
hand, there were prayers and thanksgivings for harvests
and good health; on the other, there were strict ritual practices to guard against or wash away the pollution of sickness or mortality (Sansom, 1976, p. 48). However, ethics and
morality did not figure prominently in this belief system.

  In early Japanese society, it is believed that ritual observances played an important role in daily life, and ceremonial
purification rites were part of the Shinto tradition from its
ancient beginnings. Purification, both physical and spiritual,
was stressed in order to produce a pure state of mind (*mago-
koro*, or "heart of truth," sincerity, or uprightness), which
was necessary to make contact with *kami* and to enable one
to accept the *kami's* blessing. Sansom (1976, p. 51) argues
that "the outstanding feature of Shinto observances is the
attention paid to ritual purity." Things offensive to the gods
were called *tsumi* (now guilt or sin), and avoiding these
things was called *imi*, a word meaning taboo.[3] There were
many sources of uncleanness, chief among them being dirt,

disease, and death. The word for wound, *kega*, still in use, originally meant defilement, and all external signs of disease, such as sores, eruptions, and discharges, or contact with sick persons were also thought to be defilements (ibid.).

Sakamaki (1967, p. 27) also maintains that at the core of all Shinto ceremonial is the idea of purity, and that purification was effected in various ritualistic or ceremonial ways before asking for a *kami's* blessing, including exorcism (*harai*), cleansing (*misogi*), and abstention (*imi*). Exorcism was conducted by a priest who brandished a wand in the form of a brush in front of the person to be purified while pronouncing a formula. The cleansing rite, designed to remove defilement from contact with unclean things, was effected by ablutions (i.e., ceremonial cleansing) or by the mere sprinkling of water or salt. Abstention involved avoiding contact with sickness and death (Sansom, 1976, p. 57).[4]

Mountain Torii Drawn in Ink

## CLASSIFICATION

Early Shinto in Japan can be classified into two categories: *ujigami* and *hitogami* (Hori, 1967, p. 201). The former was closely tied to the clan system and the agricultural rituals of agrarian communities;[5] the latter is linked to powerful shamanistic individuals, both male and female, who were believed to have intimate access to *kami* and the world of the spirits.

The *ujigami* type (tutelary or guardian shrine system) was based on the extended family or clan (*uji*), each having its own shrine as a central symbol of its solidarity. This type of Shinto was characterized by its particularism and exclusiveness from other families and its main function was to integrate individual family members into the group and to maintain the good name of the hereditary family (ibid., p. 202). In this system, there was a heavy emphasis on ancestor worship, filial piety (*kō*), dependence on superiors, a belief in the spirits of the dead, and the idea of an intimate connection between all humans and *kami* (ibid., p. 214.).

Shinto of the *hitogami* type, or man-god system, was based on a close relationship between an individual *kami* and a shaman, an individual believed to have the power to heal the sick and to communicate with the world beyond, and to mediate for the whole tribe with spirit world.

Early Shinto was not homogenous throughout the country, but comprised of numerous local cults, which tended to fuse and coalesce over time (Sansom, 1976, p. 50). Eventually, smaller clans expanded into larger tribal units ruled by powerful leaders. As this process took place, no distinction was made between religious and governmental ceremonies, and community leaders were both high priests and temporal rulers: "the same words were used for 'religious worship' and 'government' and for 'shrine' and 'palace'" (Reischauer, 1988, p. 42). Later, with the centralization of political power,

Shinto began to develop as a national cult as well. The myths of various clans were combined and reorganized into a pan-Japanese mythology with the Imperial Household and its *kami* at the center, and the *kami* of the powerful clans became the *kami* of the whole nation.[6]

## SHINTO SHRINES

In terms of the actual practice of Shinto, in earliest times natural phenomena such as trees, rocks, and streams were worshipped. Later, ceremonies were conducted in enclosures marked off by the branches of evergreen trees planted in the ground. Still later, Shinto shrines were built and objects such as jewels and mirrors came to symbolize the presence of *kami* (Sansom, 1976, p. 54). Shrines dedicated to various *kami* can still be found everywhere in Japan. The main one, consecrated to the Sun Goddess, stands at Ise facing the rising sun across the Pacific Ocean; numerous minor

Shrine Architecture

shrines are found at points of remarkable natural phenomena such as a great mountain, a beautiful waterfall, or simply an unusual tree or rock (Reischauer, 1988, p. 208).

Perhaps the most outstanding characteristic of Shinto
shrines is the simplicity of their construction and ornamentation. "The shrines of Ise [for example], which are pulled
down and rebuilt in exact replica every twenty years, are
thought to represent the purest and most ancient style of
Japanese architecture" (Sansom, 1976, p. 56).

Ideally, shrines are surrounded by expansive woods and
are places of a serene and solemn atmosphere in which harmony with nature is sought. Within the shrines themselves,
there is no provision made for a congregation, and only the
space for an altar and priests and attendants is needed.
Individual worshippers do not enter the shrine proper, but
stand outside to make their petition. Worship consists of
obeisance, offerings, prayers, and the clapping of hands to
attract the attention of the *kami*. Originally, offerings con-
sisted mainly of food and drink, later cloth was added, and
eventually a symbolic offering came into use in which strips
of paper representing the strips of cloth were attached to
a wand (*gohei*) and placed on the altar. It was thought that
*kami* descended into these wands, and *gohei* became objects
of worship themselves. To this day, strips of paper, cut in
a prescribed way and attached to a straw rope, confer a
special sanctity to places where they are suspended (see
Appendix E).

## THE ROLE OF SHINTO IN MODERN JAPAN

It may be thought that these early beliefs have little bear-
ing on the modern Japanese, but this would be a mistake.
Although "Shinto has slipped into a background role in
modern Japan" (Reischauer, 1988, p. 208), the truth is that
"however deeply buried under the layers of later culture, the

Torii Gate Below Mount Fuji

old conceptions have lived and operated until the present time" (Sansom, 1976, p. 48). As Sansom (ibid., p. 50) notes, "nothing is more difficult [in] early Japanese history than to distinguish what are the earliest elements in their religion, and what are later additions."

In terms of Shinto, however, it is less the early gods which are of interest, than the way ancient beliefs and customs have become embedded in modern Japanese culture. In other words, the influence of Shinto can be more readily observed in the social life of the Japanese people and in their daily routines, practices, and motivations than in any set of formal beliefs or philosophy. Shinto remains closely connected to the Japanese value system of modern times and to the Japanese people's ways of thinking and acting. Its practices can still be seen in present-day Japan in the following main areas:

(1) The continuing importance in the distinction between purity and impurity in Japanese life (*harai to kegare*):

- In essence, the "outside" is considered impure, while the "inside" is pure in Japan (see Ohnuki-Tierney, 1984, for a detailed accounting; see also Arakawa & Davies, 2001). Thus, there is the widespread practice of gargling and washing one's hands when returning home and removing one's shoes before entering a house.[7]

- The color of Shinto is white. For example, at Ise Jingu everyone wears simple, white clothing, not only priests, but also farmers, fishermen, and carpenters. The dead in Japan are dressed in white before cremation. Many workers, including taxi drivers, elevator girls, and garbage collectors, wear white gloves. Strips of white paper are used in Shinto ceremonies and tied to trees in sacred areas. People commonly wear white surgical masks when they have a cold. In the past, Japanese swordsmiths, who were considered the best in the world, wore sacred white costumes while making swords.[8]

- Water and salt are still important symbols of purification. For example, water is found in the courtyard of every temple and shrine in Japan in the form of a font for washing hands; there is a well-known indulgence for hot baths among the Japanese which is almost ritualistic in nature; salt is placed in little piles at the entrance to houses or at the edge of wells, or at the corners of the wrestling ring (*dohyō*) in Sumo; salt is also scattered on the floor after funerals, and offerings at shrines inevitably include a number of small dishes of salt, as well.

- Women's menstruation is still considered to be *kegare* (impure), and so women are barred (or used to be barred) from certain practices in Japan. For example, they are still not permitted to enter the *dohyō* in Sumo, some mountain shrines such as the one at Mt. Ishizuchi still prohibit women from attending the mountain-opening ceremony every July, and there is still a belief that pregnant women should not attend funerals.

(2) Most rites of passage in the life-cycle of the Japanese are associated with Shintoist practices:

- blessings for the newborn for a long life and good health (30–100 days old: *omiyamairi*)

- blessings again for children at ages three, five, and seven (a November holiday: *shichigosan*)

- blessings again at age 14 or 15 (associated with puberty: *shōnen-shiki* or *genpuku*)

- coming-of-age day (a January holiday for those attaining adulthood at age 20: *seijin no hi*)

- wedding ceremonies and the exchange of betrothal gifts between families (*yuino*)

- celebrations for those who reach 60 (*kanreki*), 70 (*koki*), and 88 (*beiju*) years of age

- death and dying: In Japan, almost all practices associated with death and dying, such as funerals and memorial services, are not Shintoist, but Buddhist in nature—"As a general rule, Buddhism is closely tied to matters dealing with death; funerals and memorial services for the dead are provided at its temples. Shintoism deals with birth and growth, ceremonies for births, marriage, and other matters related to growth are provided at its shrines" (Ohnuki-Tierney, 1984, p. 141). Nevertheless, there are two family altars in most homes (Shinto and Buddhist), including miniature Shinto shrines (*kamidana*) or "god shelves," where offerings are made to Shinto deities, including the spirits of family ancestors.

(3) Opening ceremonies:

- new buildings and construction sites usually undergo purification rites: *jichinsai*

Shinto Wedding Ceremony

- annual sea-opening ceremonies: *umi-biraki*

- annual ceremonies for opening mountains for hiking: *yama-biraki*

(4) Grand festivals (including the use of model shrines (*mikoshi*), purification rites (*harai*), and prayers (*norito*):

- *haru-matsuri:* asking for good crops

- *aki-matsuri:* thanks for a good harvest

- *reisai:* Annual Spirit Blessing

(5) The importance of nature and purity in literary genres and other art forms (the Japanese sense of aesthetics derives mostly from Buddhism, and this overlays the

concepts of nature and
purity which arise from
Shinto):

- in Japanese poems
  known as haiku (17
  syllables: 5-7-5) and
  *waka* (31 syllables), there are important rules for
  writing which are tied to specific key words (*kigo*)
  describing nature—e.g., *sakura* (cherry blossoms),
  *uguisu* (Japanese bush warbler)—and there are special books for writers which provide such *kigo*

- greeting cards, letters to friends and acquaintances,
  and even invitations to parents for school events in
  Japan always contain seasonal greetings, reflecting
  the changes of the four seasons (often divided into
  early and late); books of greetings are sold everywhere and provide a variety of seasonal greetings in
  the form of set phrases which have a long tradition

- analogies, allusions, and metaphors are frequently
  found in Japanese literature and nature is the most
  widely used theme; in other words, "nature" is often
  employed as a metaphor in Japanese writing, acting
  as a common cultural link and providing a kind of
  emotional bond within Japanese society

## CONCLUSION

The legacies of Shinto for present-day Japan are thus clearly
important. This inheritance is perhaps most evident in the
daily rituals and seasonal rites of the Japanese people, but
at a deeper level, the Shintoist notion of purity, in both its
positive and negative manifestations, is still one of the most

significant elements of the Japanese psyche and worldview. In addition, the belief in ancestor worship, the spirits of the dead, and the idea of an intimate connection between men and *kami* remains widespread in modern Japan. Finally, the worship of natural objects has its counterpart in a delicate sensibility and strong awareness of the beauty of nature in Japanese life: "The Japanese love of nature and sense of closeness to it also derive strongly from Shinto concepts" (Reischauer, 1988, p. 211). Since ancient times the Japanese have found symbols of *kami* in natural objects and the forces of nature, and in so doing they developed an explicitly religious poetry, as well as an architecture and a variety of art forms to express this appreciation. In these literary and artistic endeavors is illustrated the fundamental Japanese preference for emotional and aesthetic intuitions in expressing their religious and philosophical experiences, perhaps Shinto's most important legacy.

## NOTES

1. Shotoku Taishi (573–621 AD) was crown prince and regent of Japan from 593 AD until his death. He was perhaps the most influential ruler of ancient Japan. He sent envoys to China and imported Chinese artists, craftsmen, and clerks into Japan in order to remodel the Japanese state after China. He wrote the constitution that prepared the way for the Taika reform and he promoted Buddhism and Confucianism in what had previously been an exclusively Shinto culture. He erected many Buddhist temples, including what has become the oldest wooden structure in the world, the Horyuji Temple in Nara.

2. Animism, after the Greek word *anima*, meaning "soul" or "breath," was one of the earliest manifestations of human religious awareness. People believed in a world where "spirit

beings" inhabited animals, rocks, trees, weapons, orna-
ments, and so forth. Shamanism, a term primarily applied
to the belief systems of north Asian, Siberian, and native
American Indian peoples, is a kind of applied animism,
or animism in practice. A shaman's spirit is thought to be
able to enter the bodies of other people, animals, or objects:
"Because Nature is alive with gods and spirits, and because
all aspects of the cosmos are perceived as interconnected—
the universe consisting of a veritable network of energies,
forms and vibrations—the shaman is required as an inter-
mediary between the different planes of being" (Drury, 1989,
p. 5). The shaman is thus "a person who is able to perceive
this world of souls, spirits, and gods, and who, in a state of
ecstatic trance, is able to travel among them, gaining special
knowledge of that supernatural realm" (ibid., p. 6). Miko, or
shamanesses, are still sometimes found in small villages in
Japan, where they utilize trance, mediumship, and fortune-
telling and communicate with guardian deities or spirits of
the dead.

3. Eating meat was not originally taboo, but appears to
have become so under later Buddhist influence. Intoxicating
liquors, however, were not taboo and figured prominently in
offerings to the kami (Sansom, 1976, p. 57).

4. Of note is the fact that this feeling of contamination
through association with the sick or disabled is a source of
great suffering for many in Japan. Numerous recent reports
in the mass media have detailed the plight of AIDS patients
(Ono, 1995, p. 12), many of whom are forced to move to
other countries to die, as well as those suffering from lep-
rosy (Hansen's disease), who were kept in complete isolation until quite recently, but three decades after this kind
of seclusion was supposedly warranted (Kumeta, 1996, p. 6).

5.  Shinto festivals, for example, are believed to have originated with agricultural rites which became mixed with
ancestor worship and a belief in the spirits of the dead. The
physical world at this time was considered to be tripartite—
the ethereal firmament above, the surface of the earth as
the human abode, and the shadowy nether regions down
below. After dying, individuals were believed to join an
extended family of ancestral spirits, and the dead person's
spirit was thought to lose its identity 33 years after death,
when it would then join this community of ancestral spirits. Buddhist memorial services to a personal spirit (Buddhism took over a number of originally Shinto functions) are
stopped at the 33rd anniversary service called *tomuraiage* or
*toikiri*. After this, the spirit of the dead is believed to become
an ancestral spirit (Hori, 1967, p. 220).

6.  Though early Shinto was in essence nature worship, it
developed in special directions under official auspices, and
it is important to distinguish the traditional body of popular
belief from the institutional religion fostered by the government. The former was simple ritualism based on an animistic creed and colored by magic; the latter was organized
and bound up with the political system (Sansom, 1976, p.
54). As Shinto developed, it was greatly influenced by powerful new forces imported to Japan in the forms of Confucianism, Taoism, and Buddhism, and for many centuries
Shintoist beliefs were colored by the influences of these
great traditions. In modern times, Shinto was fused with
the Imperial State in the Meiji era, and because it became
associated with nationalistic and militaristic tendencies,
State Shinto was disbanded after World War II. The folk tradition, however, continues to live on in the values and daily
practices of the Japanese people. In addition, the relationship of Shinto to later-arriving religious beliefs in Japan was

generally marked by harmony and cooperation, and these qualities have become key elements in the religious and philosophical attitudes of the Japanese people today.

7. In Japan, students gargle (*ugai*) and wash their hands several times a day: "After bathroom breaks, everyone washes their hands together, out in the hall where teachers can supervise. Students wash up again before lunch, after science experiments, and when they come in from recess. In most homes, kids are expected to wash their hands as soon as they come home . . ., [and] gargle, too." In fact, dozens of schools in Japan "post information on their gargling programs," while some schools have "the kids march to the sinks for a group gargle" to the accompaniment of music on the public address system (Gordenker, 2003, p. 17). However, as numerous newspaper articles recount, many people in Japan, especially the young, seem to be growing phobic about germs: "the most fastidious country in the world is becoming even more hygiene-obsessed" (Efron, 1996, p. 9). Japanese consumers today have over 600 antibacterial products to choose from, including computer keyboards, car steering wheels, toilet seats, and disposable karaoke microphones. Inada Nada, a Japanese child psychologist, maintains that "people harbor the subconscious belief that anyone they dislike is unclean. . . . The Japanese concepts of *yogore*, or dirtiness, and *kegare*, a spiritual taint or defilement, tend to merge in people's minds" (ibid.).

8. The importance of the color white for the Japanese could be seen in the recent past in a lengthy dispute between the All Japan Judo Federation and International Judo Federation, until the Japanese finally conceded. European judo officials, in particular, wanted to introduce the use of colored judo uniforms to make the sport more appealing and easier to understand for the general public, as well as to enhance

television coverage. The Japanese were fiercely opposed to this change and had a long-standing preference for the color white "which is said to represent the purity of the sport" (Yata, 1996, p. 7).

## DISCUSSION ACTIVITIES

1. It is said that in Shinto there is a sense of awe and reverence before nature, but there is no definite idea of a soul, no clear distinction between life and death, nor between body and spirit. Do modern Japanese people still have a sense of awe and reverence before nature? What is your definition of "soul"?

2. Numerous critics have pointed out that the reverence of nature depicted in Japanese writing is extremely difficult to reconcile with the country's reputation as one of the world's consummate wreakers of environmental destruction. Alex Kerr, author of *Lost Japan* and winner of Japan's prestigious *Shincho Gakugei* Literature Prize, claims that the systematic destruction of the natural environment by the Japanese has resulted in Japan achieving "a position as one of the world's ugliest countries," and that apart from certain showpiece areas, "Japan's countryside has been utterly defiled" by dioxins, toxic waste, overfishing, forest destruction, and so on (1996, p. 49). On the Internet, do some research on environmental destruction in Japan. As a result of your research, do you agree with Kerr's depiction of Japan, or do you think his criticisms are overstated? Why, or why not?

3. In the West, things are often perceived in terms of dichotomies, such as body vs. spirit, right vs. wrong, man vs. nature, life vs. death, etc. On the other hand, in animistic beliefs, everything, from natural phenomena to human beings and their ancestors, are treated as an integral part of

the whole. What do you think about this difference in the way we perceive the world?

4. Hansen's disease patients are not the only people who have been deprived of their human rights in Japan. There have also been reports in the mass media of hospitals refusing to treat people with Minamata disease, as well as discrimination against *hibaskusha* (elderly sufferers of atomic radiation). In addition, institutions for the physically and mentally handicapped are often built far from city centers in isolated areas that are difficult to reach. Discuss these forms of discrimination in terms of Shinto's emphasis on the importance of ritual purity.

5. Many people in Japan go to a Shinto shrine to pray for success before a big event in their lives. For example, students who are going to take an entrance test often pray for success at a shrine and may also buy *omamori* (a talisman or charm). There is a proverb that says "*kurushii toki no kami-danomi*" ("people only pray to the gods when they are in trouble"). Discuss the role of prayer in Shinto.

6. There is a long history of multiple belonging to religions in Japan. According to the Agency for Cultural Affairs, 90% of Japanese people profess a belief in Shinto and 75% in Buddhism. Most people have an association with both. What roles do these religions play in the lives of the Japanese? What is the role of other religions such as Christianity?

7. It is important to note that, although there has been considerable blending of religious elements in Japan, most Japanese draw important distinctions among them, especially in terms of ritual practices involving Shinto and Buddhism. For example, there is the common practice of marking the change in the status of the deceased from buddha to god

at the final memorial service after a long period of purification of the spirit (normally on the thirty-third or fiftieth anniversary of death). At this time, the memorial tablet is moved from the Buddhist altar in the house and some form of substitute is placed on the god shelf. Moreover, gods and buddhas are enshrined separately in most Japanese homes:

> The god shelf (*kamidama*) is high up on the wall of the room, often above a door, and is made of untreated wood. It contains no images, for the gods are not anthropomorphized. The worshiper stands before it. The Buddhist altar, by contrast, is usually an ornately lacquered and gilded cabinet set into or against a wall. It may contain a representation of the Buddha; it almost invariably contains memorial tablets of the dead. Ordinarily the worshiper sits before it. When there is a severe illness or death in the household, it is still today the common practice to seal off the god shelf lest the pollution offend the gods and bring harm to the members of the family. (Smith, 1974, p. 3)

In what other ways do the Japanese draw distinctions between Shinto and Buddhism?

8. *Religions in Japan* describes Shinto practices in prehistoric antiquity as follows:

> The worshipper in prehistoric antiquity usually faced the object of devotion itself, which might be a tree, stone, mountain, or sunrise. He performed his devotions standing within a sacred enclosure, which was often set within a quiet grove. In time, a shrine was erected at the spot, or, if the object of worship was a distant mountain, only a covering was prepared under which the worshipper might stand. The shrines were always of extremely

simple construction with no decorative effects, usually nothing more than a thatched roof supported by straight pillars. (Bunce, 1955, p. 39)

Do some research on Ise Jingu, Japan's most sacred shrine. Describe how it was built, its architectural structure, what people working there wear, and any other interesting characteristics that are related to Shinto.

9. In the past, most Japanese people got married in Shinto ceremonies. However, recent reports in the mass media state that approximately two-thirds of Japanese couples are currently opting for "chapel marriages." Why? What does this mean for Shinto?

# Buddhism

## INTRODUCTION

If Shinto can be thought of as the bedrock layer in our conceptual model illustrating the formative elements of Japanese culture, Buddhism would have to be considered the next stratum of religious and philosophical belief. Buddhism, which has been the spiritual foundation of Japanese culture for centuries, not only had a seminal influence on Japanese aesthetic expression in literature, architecture, theater, and the visual arts, but it also carried within it the values, ways of thinking, and social and political institutions of continental China (Reischauer, 1988; Sansom, 1976). As such, one of Buddhism's most significant roles in Japanese history was as a vehicle for the transmission of a whole higher culture and civilization, that of classical China.

## BUDDHIST DOCTRINE

Buddhism originates with the teachings of the historical Buddha (the "Enlightened One" or the "Awakened One") in 5th century BC India. As a religious belief system, it discourages both philosophical theorizing and metaphysical speculation: truth lies beyond rational analysis and can be understood only by someone who has walked on the path and reported what he has seen (i.e., a Buddha). Buddhist doctrine can be thought of as a vehicle which comes in many different forms: it is typically compared to a ferryboat, which, after being used to cross the river of life from the shore of worldly experience, spiritual ignorance, and suffering to the farther shore of transcendental wisdom, is discarded once the other side is reached.

Buddhism stresses that life is painful and that its suffering derives from human attachment or desires. Desire and attachment cause suffering because what is desired is transitory, changing, and perishable: the impermanence of the object of our desire is what causes disappointment and sorrow. The Buddha taught that people can be freed from this suffering by following his teachings, which are based on four noble truths and an eightfold path that emphasizes a middle way and avoids the extremes of both hedonism and asceticism. The aim of Buddhist religious practice is to free oneself from the chains of the mundane world in order to overcome a never-ending cycle of birth and rebirth by achieving Enlightenment, a painless merging with the cosmos in *nirvana* (or "nothingness"). Buddhism teaches that the only true reality is one's innermost soul (or *atman*, a concept derived from Hindu beliefs), outside of which everything is temporal, fleeting, changing, and unreal. This awareness that everything will unfailingly pass away helps to induce a serenity of spirit among its believers.

Buddhism has never had a centralized authority and teaches an individualistic ethical morality which places autonomous value on one's actions; i.e., good is good for its own sake. Buddhist ethics emphasize a middle way, but offer no mandatory dogma nor specific injunctions—obstinant attachment to one point of view, good or bad, is discouraged. Compassion is Buddhism's central ethical principle, and charity, hospitality, an ideal love of all living things, and internal purification are also considered important. It is said that there are two pillars on which the Buddhist life is built: compassion and detachment (to be detached is to be free; to be free leads to equanimity). There is no belief in a divine creator in Buddhism, but it is thought that universal laws called *dharmas* govern human existence and human actions should be brought into harmony with them. The universe itself is seen as uncreated, without beginning or end: origination, duration, and annihilation succeed one another in recurrent cyclic change. Buddhism presupposes laws of karma and the transmigration of souls which are reborn in accordance with one's worldly deeds. However, these metaphysical matters are not stressed in Buddhism—its essential concern is human conduct.[1]

Thus, the aim of Buddhism is not, "as in Western religions, to define and worship a Creator God" (the Buddha never denied the existence of gods, but he did not like speaking about them). Nor is the highest goal "to ensure access to some kind of heaven after death." What the Buddha sought was "an Exit"—"a final and total release from cyclic existence," which is called *nirvana* or enlightenment (Snelling, 1990, p. 5). In other words, the Buddha himself was not very concerned with offering "dogmatic formulations" but rather with "helping people to see the Truth and find liberation for themselves" (ibid., p. 6).

## INTRODUCTION OF BUDDHISM IN JAPAN

Buddhism arrived in Japan a thousand years after its long journey from India through the countries of East Asia as it penetrated toward the outer extremities of the Pacific rim (see Appendix F). At this time, there had long been a steady flow of cultural influences into Japan from the continent, and in the 6th century AD the flow began to increase, bringing with it the new Buddhist beliefs from the continent (Reischauer, 1988).

When Buddhism arrived, Japan did not have any genuine system of religious speculation—Shinto was dominant, and Buddhism had to define itself in relation to Shinto. Initially, the magico-religious character of Buddhist rites and readings of sacred texts appealed to the people, and Buddhism in Japan became colored at first by magical practices. D. H. Suzuki (as cited in Snelling, 1990, p. 32) describes the Buddhism of the Heian period, for example, as "flooded with magical ritualism."

Inevitably, conflict with existing social patterns arose and resulted in a dispute at the central Yamato court over the acceptance of Buddhist images and beliefs as a magical system of equal or even greater power than Shinto. Eventually, a symbiosis developed between the two: Shinto shrines were often found in Buddhist temples, and Buddhism accepted local divinities and made them objects of worship, adopting many kami in this way. Buddhism and Shinto eventually accommodated themselves to each other, and as Buddhism adapted to Japan, to Shinto, and to the emotional and aesthetic life of the Japanese people, it was modified with many of the qualities of early Japanese traditions (Sansom, 1976).

Japanese Buddhism was thus transformed into the spiritual foundation of the clan system, and ancestor worship became one of its prime functions (a present-day example is the Buddhist holiday, O-bon, when many Japanese visit their ancestral homes in order to pay respect to the spirits of their ancestors who are thought to return at this time). In its beginnings, Buddhism was seen simply as a means of protecting the emperor against calamities and diseases, and so acted as a talisman for protection of the nation. In the course of time, however, the laws of karma and rebirth were accepted, funeral rites were altered, religious schools were

Golden Pavilion, Kinkakuji

introduced, and Buddhism became a principal component of Japanese thought.

The adoption of both Buddhism and the Chinese political system by the Yamato court in the early 7th century is attributed to a Japanese statesman named Prince Shotoku. Shotoku himself wrote commentaries on Buddhist scriptures, built Buddhist monasteries, dispatched embassies to the Chinese capital, and drafted a constitution embodying both Buddhist and Confucian precepts. He is credited with the 17 Article Constitution, which was of great importance in the early state-building period, and the first document of its kind in Japanese history. In this constitution there is a clear assertion of the central authority at Yamato, but there are also extraordinary qualifications of this authority, with other strands of Chinese and non-Chinese thought woven into its loose fabric. Synthesis and consensus are its primary values, not the assertion of one tradition over another. This process of consensus formation through the use of consultation continued in the family, clan, and state councils that have played a key role, often behind the scenes, in Japanese affairs through the ages, and expresses the essence of the

Sensoji

Japanese political process (Reischauer, 1988). In Shotoku's work, three elements met: Shinto, Confucian ethics, and Buddhism. The 17 Articles are considered a unique product of native traditions in dialogue with continental philosophies, and illustrate an early Japanese disposition to reconcile opposing forces through the consultative process.

## THE THREE MAIN STREAMS OF JAPANESE BUDDHISM

In China at this time, the rapprochement of Buddhism and the Chinese dynastic state had become a model for all East Asia of a religion legitimizing the ruler and the ruler patronizing the religion without any genuine exchange between the two.[2] Buddhism left no residual influence on the Chinese political tradition, and from the 8th century onward, it began to suffer a decline in China (Buddhism also went into decline in India at around the same time, and by the 13th century it essentially ceased to exist in that country). As the great monastic institutions lost power in China, new forms of religious practice, de-emphasizing doctrine, took their place. Of these, Pure Land devotionalism and the practice of Ch'an (Zen) meditation are the most representative of later Chinese Buddhism. Both were adopted by Japan and had a lasting influence there.[3]

As Buddhism gradually became absorbed into the cultural fabric of Japanese life, it developed "three major emphases" (Reischauer, 1988, p. 206). The first, as noted above, was an "esoteric" Buddhism which stressed magic formulas, rituals, and art.[4] The second, which started in the 10th century, was based on salvation through faith, particularly in Amida, the Buddha of the "Pure Land" of the Western Paradise, and resulted in the founding of new sects in the 12th and 13th centuries: the Pure Land Sect (Jōdo-shū), the True Pure Land Sect (Jōdo Shin-shū),[5] and Nichiren,[6] the three largest Buddhist sects today in Japan. The basic doctrines of Pure Land differed widely from those of early Buddhism, especially in the belief that salvation was not obtainable by individual effort or accumulation of merit, but only by faith in the grace of Amida Buddha, who waits in the Pure Land, also known as the Western Paradise, and helps believers achieve salvation. The main practice was neither meditation nor the study of texts, but constant invocation and chanting of the name of Amida (*nembutsu*). The goal was not Enlightenment, but to become reborn in the Pure Land, where no evil exists, people are long-lived and receive whatever they desire, and from where they might attain *nirvana*. Reischauer (ibid., p. 60) describes this evolution of Buddhist doctrine as follows:

> The court aristocrats had been most interested in a form of Buddhism that emphasized magic formulas and rituals, but during the eleventh and twelfth centuries a new emphasis developed, especially among more plebeian Japanese. This was belief in salvation and entrance into paradise through simple faith—that is, through reliance on the grace of one of the many Buddhist deities. Such concepts were an almost complete reversal of the original Buddhist doctrine of the merging of the personal ego into the cosmos through austere self-cultivation leading to enlightenment.

The third emphasis in Japan was on self-reliance in seeking salvation through self-discipline and meditation, known today as Zen Buddhism. Because Zen, in its Chinese form of Ch'an Buddhism, was so strongly influenced by Taoist thought, and because it plays such a pivotal role in the development and refinement of Japanese culture and aesthetics, it will be examined in more detail later, after an introduction to the influence of Taoism on Japanese thought.

Nyonin-do, Mt. Koya

## THE EVOLUTION OF BUDDHISM IN JAPAN

Of great importance for understanding the historic role of
Buddhism in Japan is the fact that it not only became the
spiritual core of Japanese life, influencing many forms of
cultural and aesthetic expression, but it was also tailor-
made as a vehicle for the transmission of a higher civilization to Japan, that of ancient China (Burns & Ralph, 1965;
Reischauer, 1988; Sansom, 1976). Buddhism was a meditative religion, but although it was inward-looking, it looked
inward at no center. With its emphasis on the principles of
impermanence, illusion, and the truth of Enlightenment, it
had no structured, definable nature. Buddhism was also a
preaching or missionary religion, but it looked outward on
the world with no fixed center of authority. There were no
fixed principles to be implemented in the world, no affirma-
tion of defined values that could lead to social and political
opposition. As a result, Buddhism was free on reaching East
Asia to shed its Indian garments and pick up new cultural
baggage and carry it forward. It followed this pattern of cul-

tural adaptation in each country in which it was introduced, and in the process it helped bring to Japan much of the classical legacy of ancient China in the form of Confucian and Taoist philosophy, literature, and the arts, as well as Han ideas and political institutions, and even a writing system (*kanji*) in which this new knowledge could be recorded.

When Buddhism arrived in Japan it was thus not seen as an expansion of Chinese power and influence but primarily as an extension of Buddhism's progress across East Asia. This occurred at a time of political fragmentation and cultural disorientation in China and of rapid historical change in Japan. At the dawning of civilized life in Japan (i.e., literate, citified society), Japan's own indigenous traditions were polycentric, particularistic, and strongly hierarchical. At this time, Buddhism contributed greatly to the process of state-building because of its spiritual dynamism and adaptability to new situations.

The branch of Buddhism that spread throughout East Asia is called Mahayana, or the "greater vehicle," in contrast to Theravada, the "doctrine of the elders" (or "lesser vehicle"), which survived in much of southeast Asia (see Appendix F). It came to stress reverence for the "Three Treasures": (1) the Buddha, (2) the teachings embodied in a vast Buddhist literature, and (3) the religious community, or monastic organizations. In addition, there is a reverence for *bodhisattvas*, or beings who have reached Enlightenment but have decided to stay back one step from *nirvana* in order to aid in the salvation of others (in Japan, they are represented in Buddhist temples

Jizō Figures

by small statues known as o-jizō-sama, or "earth-god statues," thus again reflecting Shinto influences).

Early Buddhism had stressed the necessity of a monastic life in order to provide an environment in which practitioners would be able to follow the disciplines necessary
for the attainment of their ethical ideals and for Enlightenment. This "otherworldly" stance was preserved in Theravada, in which a monastic order was central. Mahayana
scholars, however, maintained that moral disciplines could
be followed and that the Absolute could be comprehended
in secular life. This latter point of view was selected by the
Japanese, who have always stamped their Buddhist doctrines with a "this-worldliness." Reclusiveness and non-
attachment were repudiated by the early Japanese, who
put heavy emphasis upon activity in human relationships,
and this accounts for the absence of all-inclusive monastic
orders in Japan. Furthermore, the Japanese generally disap-
proved of begging and permitted the marriage of priests,
who also had close contact with the common people. Ethical
values associated with productive labor and hard work were
also stressed, as well as engagement in community work
through hospitals, orphanages, and schools. The Theravada
monks were not allowed to engage in economic activities,
cultivate land, or make profit (they had to live on alms);
in Japan, the spirit of labor and service became strongly
emphasized (Reischauer, 1988).

The Japanization of Buddhism evolved gradually, and as
it did so, Buddhist religious theory became simplified and
rationalized, more emphasis was put on faith and devotion
and practices related to daily life, and excessive speculation
and theorizing were discouraged. Japanese Buddhist scholars have tended to produce quantities of writing which are
essentially practical in nature and quite unlike the highly
analytical philosophy of earlier Indian Buddhists. In addition, the qualities of sectarianism (i.e., factionalism) and

nationalism which are found in Japanese Buddhism are generally not present in the Buddhism of other countries. The reclusive, monastic, inward-looking Theravada tradition was rejected, as Mahayana doctrines, which advocated comprehending absolute truth from within secular life and the necessity of realizing Buddhist ideals within concrete human situations, suited the indigenous social patterns of the Japanese. The Buddhism of Japan, like that of China, was thus pragmatic and "this-worldly." Monasteries operated stores, built roads, engaged in commerce, and set up schools. They even introduced the popular Japanese custom of bathing by opening the baths used in monasteries for daily purification practices to the common people, and the traditional Japanese diet (*shōjin ryori*) also originated in Zen monasteries. In this way, Buddhism promoted a social consciousness that encompassed all classes of people and promised salvation for all mankind. This social concern was expressed in the building of temples that served as centers of philanthropic and cultural activity for the whole nation.

After the adoption of Buddhism in the 6th century and a vigorous borrowing of all things Chinese for two centuries more, the flow tapered off in the 9th century. From the 9th to the 16th centuries, Buddhism "permeated the whole intellectual, artistic, and social life of Japan," transforming the country from a backward, tribal region into a full participant in a higher civilization (Reischauer, 1988, p. 206). Buddhism in its many forms transformed Japanese life in myriad ways. It was first and foremost the vehicle by which classical Chinese civilization was carried to Japan; it also had a deep and lasting effect on both the spiritual and aesthetic life of the Japanese people. Buddhism continued to be the dominant force in Japan well into the 16th century, at which time Confucianism rose to ascendancy as the official philosophy of the Tokugawa shogunate.[7]

## NOTES

1. In order to understand Buddhism, it is important to have a clear idea of the cosmology from which Buddhist doctrine originated. Snelling (1990, p. 4) states that the early Buddhists believed in views of the universe that were generally held in India at that time, and fundamental to these views is the idea that "time is not linear but circular." As a result, the universe "has always existed and will always exist, but it goes through endless cycles of creation and destruction." Anyone born into this cyclic universe is the result of something that has gone before; in Buddhist terms, "he or she is the fruit of a preceding cause or willed action (karma)." In other words, we are all links in "an endless circular spiralling chain that reaches back into the beginningless past and forward into the endless future." The words to describe this process of souls moving along the chain of being are "transmigration" and "rebirth" (ibid.).

2. Buddhism in China reached the height of its power and influence during the Sui and T'ang Dynasties (581–907 AD). By that time, "a fully Sinicised Buddhism had emerged, forged by the creative interaction of Indian teachings with local traditions, notably Taoism" (ibid., p. 31). Four of the many schools of Buddhism that flourished in this period were distinctly Chinese, and two of them—the Pure Land School and Ch'an (or Zen)—were eventually passed on to Japan.

3. The Pure Land and Ch'an (Zen) traditions are illustrative of the two main streams that have always existed in Buddhist history as paths to salvation, the devotional approach and the path of inner knowledge and insight. The former is considered the easier route, one suitable for the common people; the latter is thought to be a more difficult path, but truer.

4. There were six schools of Buddhism in the Nara period (646–794 AD), but all were highly scholastic and their sphere of influence was limited to monks and did not extend to the common people (Risshū, Kusha, Jōjitsu, Sanron, Hossō, and Kegon). The Kegon sect provided the ideology for a Buddhist state in the Nara period with its doctrine of the interpenetration of all things. Buddhism during the Heian period (794–1185 AD) developed in a period of intense co-mingling of diverse religious elements, including traditional Buddhist doctrines, religious Taoism, and primitive shamanism. During this period, the Tendai and Shingon sects became prominent. The Tendai school was based on the Lotus sutra and taught that all people can become Buddhas and should attempt to do so. It was comprehensive in that it found a place for all the Buddhist scriptures. Shingon was introduced to Japan by Kūkai (or Kōbō Daishi), and the term itself means "true word" (or mantra). It is interfused with magical elements from India and central Asia, as well as native elements, and is a form of esoteric Buddhism (esoteric: obscure knowledge restricted to a small group). It represents a synthesis of philosophies and is known for being tolerant towards other faiths. During the

Kamakura period (1185–1392 AD), the aristocracy declined and the military class rose to ascendancy. Many Buddhist sects degenerated into meaningless esoteric and magical practices, and warfare and strife were everywhere, creating great distress for many people; as a result, there was a need for a simplified religious outlook. At the turn of 13th century, Zen was introduced from China, the Pure Land sects became prominent, and new schools such as

Kōbō Daishi

Nichiren arose. Thereafter, there were no new sects in Japan until Meiji times. The Buddhist sects that are still extant are Tendai, Shingon, Zen, Pure Land, and Nichiren.

5. Pure Land Buddhism was founded in 1st and 2nd century India (the Pure Land sutra was written in India in the 2nd century AD) and started to become prominent in Japan in the 12th century. The Pure Land (Jōdo) is also known as the Western Paradise, where believers are reborn after death. Amida Buddha (the former Indian monk, Dharmakara) sits in this land helping people achieve salvation—he is known as the Buddha of Unlimited Light (Amida). Pure Land stresses faith in Amida's grace, and people can be reborn into the Western Paradise by virtue of this faith and by their good works. Pure Land was originally brought to Japan by the Tendai sect in Heian times as they tried to weld the many Japanese Buddhist sects into one. By the Kamakura period, Pure Land had split off and spread to common people mainly through the work of Hōnen and Shinran, although Genkū is credited with being the founder of the Jōdo sect. Pure Land originally placed emphasis on good works, but later forms stressed faith and devotion alone. *Nirvana* is not the immediate goal, but rather, one will later attain *nirvana* by first becoming reborn in the Pure Land. Hōnen founded the Pure Land sect (Jōdo-shū), and Shinran founded the True Pure Land sect (Jōdo Shin-shū), which is more radical and requires only absolute faith in the grace of Amida. Today, Pure Land sects are the most popular form of Buddhism in Japan, and they continue to stress the deep-rootedness of sin in the human condition, that all human beings are karma-bound, and that salvation can be achieved by the grace of Amida Buddha.

6. The Nichiren sect was founded by the prophet and nationalist Nichiren in the 13th century. Although trained

in the Tendai school, he decided that only one scripture was needed, the Lotus sutra. He became a religious demagogue and preached with great fervour, attacking other sects and reinterpreting the Lotus sutra to give people peace and salvation. Later, Sōka Gakkai became the political arm of Nichiren Buddhism, stressing action according to things (i.e., the phenomenal world) rather than action according to principles (as with the Tendai school).

7. Many elements of classical Confucianism entered Japan with the first great wave of Chinese influence between the sixth and ninth centuries, but "Confucianism tended to be overshadowed by Buddhism until the emergence of the centralized Tokugawa system in the seventeenth century. . . . From then on, Confucian schools of philosophy dominated thought and Confucian attitudes pervaded society" (Reischauer, 1988, pp. 203–204).

## DISCUSSION ACTIVITIES

1. It is said that many Japanese do not believe in any religion. Yet people generally follow important Buddhist and Shinto rituals at certain times of the year even if they do not believe in them. Why?

2. Why was Buddhism so readily accepted in Japan in the 6th century when an indigenous religion in the form of Shinto already existed?

3. After the Buddha died, Buddhism gradually split into two schools: Theravada (or Hinayana), literally "the doctrine of the elders" (or "the lesser vehicle"), and Mahayana, literally "the greater vehicle." The former focuses on self-enlightenment and became established in a number of southeast Asian countries (e.g., Sri Lanka, Burma, Thailand, Laos, and

Cambodia), while the latter is concerned with enlightening oneself as well as others, preaching social concern and universal salvation, and spread north through China and Korea to Japan. Why was Mahayana Buddhism more readily accepted by the Japanese than Theravada Buddhism?

4. How do the Japanese distinguish between Buddhism and Shinto? What differences exist in the way they are practiced in Japan, especially in terms of events such as festivals, rituals, etc.?

5. Although both Buddhism and Shinto have had major influences on Japanese culture, many modern Japanese seem know little about religion in general. Why is this? In school, how are religions taught in Japan? What do school children learn about this aspect of Japanese culture? Discuss education in Japan from this point of view, particularly from a historical perspective.

6. In Shikoku, Kūkai established 88 temples for pilgrims as holy places in the 7th century. It was only for monks at first, and then this pilgrimage became popular among ordinary people during the Muromachi to Edo eras. Around the same time, it became popular with people who were socially alienated, had incurable diseases, or were beggars. Since people in Shikoku were accustomed to providing pilgrims with food and money as a contribution (o-settai) to the pilgrimage, it was easy for them to travel. Even today, many people visit Shikoku for this reason. Although there are many bus tours, the number of people who visit all the temples on foot (called aruki henro) is also increasing. What do you think the meaning of this pilgrimage is for Japanese people today?

7. Many Westerners come to Japan with the image of Buddhism as a contemplative religion which involves a great deal

of meditation and aims for self-realization. How does this image compare with the way the Japanese view Buddhism?

8. Although Zen Buddhism is not the largest sect in Japan, it is the most popular and widely recognized in the West. Why is it not as popular as other Buddhist sects in Japan?

9. Over the past few decades, a number of celebrities in the West have converted to Buddhism; e.g., Richard Gere, Michelle Pfeiffer, and Phil Jackson (coach of the Chicago Bulls and Los Angeles Lakers). What do you think attracted these people to Buddhism?

10. What does the following Buddhist saying mean?: "Enlightenment is attained by awakening to the truth."

11. Discuss the Japanese perspective on an afterlife. How does it compare with the beliefs of other people in the world?

12. Do you consider modern Japan to be a spiritual place? Why, or why not ?

13. Japanese people frequently visit their family graves, following Buddhist rituals related to death and dying; for instance, they visit on the day of the spring or fall equinox, the Bon festival, and the monthly and yearly anniversaries of the death of closely related family members. Do these kinds of customs exist in other countries? How are they similar or different?

14. Buddhism stresses the importance of a lack of material possessions. Yet, in modern Japan, as in many other places in the world, materialism is rampant. How can this be reconciled with Buddhist principles?

# Taoism

## INTRODUCTION

Taoism and Confucianism are considered to be the two main religious and philosophical traditions of China. Taoism affected Japanese culture mostly as a result of its formative influences on Zen Buddhism, while classical Confucianism entered Japan in earlier waves of influence, along with Buddhism, and became the official doctrine of the Tokugawa shogunate in its later form of neo-Confucianism.

Taoist divination techniques and other magico-religious practices were introduced into Japan starting in the 6th century along with numerous other borrowings from ancient China, and "although Taoism has never been institutionalized in Japan, it has penetrated deeply into folk belief systems and practices" (Ohnuki-Tierney, 1984, p. 135). Taoism is still found in modern Japan, and Japanese scholarship on the Taoist tradition is considered one of the foremost in the world.

"Tao" literally means "way," but also *the* Way to be followed, and by extension, a code of behavior and doctrine (cf. *dō* in Japanese). Many Japanese expressions contain the *kanji dō* (道), and these words carry a wide range of meanings, from the mundane to the profound. The following are examples of some of the ways in which *dō* can be used in Japanese:

- *dōkyō*: Taoism
- *dōro*: street or road
- *dōtoku*: morals
- *kadō*: flower arrangement (*ikenbana*)
- *shodō*: calligraphy
- *kendō*: swordsmanship
- judo: "the soft way"
- Shinto: "the way of the gods"
- *dōjō*: practice room
- *dōraku*: entertainment
- *bushidō*: "the way of the warrior"
- *sadō*: tea ceremony
- *kyūdō*: archery
- aikido: meeting/energy/way

## TAOIST BELIEFS

Taoism is said to have originated with the ideas of Lao Tzu in 5th century BC China, who taught that the notion of Tao expresses the unity of man and nature. Taoism thus became involved in techniques aimed at bringing Heaven and Earth together; i.e., blending the sacred powers of the heavens with ritual practice in the mundane world. According to Lao Tzu, all things have their origin in the interaction of the two opposites of Yin and Yang: "Two gives birth to the three" (Palmer, 1991, p. 5). This is the triad of Heaven, Earth, and Humanity, which is the form by which all living things come into existence.

On another level, mystical Tao is also a universal force of the cosmos: "the Tao that cannot be named," or that which lies at the origin of the universe and behind or within appearances. In this sense, the universe is viewed as a hierarchically organized mechanism in which each part reproduces the whole—the individual human being is a microcosm (small universe) corresponding rigorously to the macrocosm (large universe), and the human body is thought to reproduce the plan of the cosmos.

The law of the Tao refers to the continuous reversion of everything to its starting point; in other words, anything that develops extreme qualities will invariably revert to its opposite. Life and death are contained in this eternal transformation from Non-Being into Being and back to Non-Being, but the underlying primordial unity (the Tao that cannot be named) is never lost.

The Taoist view of creation is that all parts of the universe are attuned to a rhythmical pulsation, nothing is static, and all life is subject to periodic transformations. These changes were systematized and made intelligible as a theory of divination in the I Ching (The Book of Changes) in which 64 hexagrams based on Yin and Yang principles illustrate basic recurrent constellations in the general flux[1] (see Appendix G). The alternations of Yin and Yang, or opposing energies (seen as female and male, night and day, good and bad, winter and summer, and so forth), is nothing but the external aspect of the same Tao. Yin and Yang are often referred to as the two "breaths"; i.e., cosmic energy or ch'i (from prana in Sanskrit; cf. ki in Japanese).

A distinct lack of any speculative thought is characteristic of Taoism, nor is there any sense of a creator god. There are no theologians in the Western sense and few philosophers as in Buddhism. Of the major religions of the world, Taoism is the one with the least rationalization, in which the communication of man with the sacred appears in its most immediate and unreflective form. The individual who wants to know the Tao is told: "Don't meditate, don't cogitate, discard knowledge, forget distinctions, follow no school, and then you will attain the Tao" (Tao Te Ching). In other words, "to understand anything about the philosophy of the Tao, you really need to be in a state of wise ignorance" (Watts, 1997, p. 18).

It is said that the Tao cannot be grasped, but it can be received. Under a master "teaching without words,"[2] the

adept goes through a cathartic process of emptying the
mind of all passions and distinctions until it becomes a
"mirror of Heaven and Earth reflecting the multiplicity of
things." The person then becomes inhabited by the Tao and
finally reaches enlightenment through an experience outside of time and space and being in the eternal now.

## TAOIST PRACTICES

In essence, the Taoist seeks to follow the Path or the Way
of the Tao "in order to achieve unity with the Ultimate Tao
beyond the One. To do this, Taoism has devised a vast array
of methods and ways, [which] fall into the following broad
categories": *wu-wei* (the concept of non-action), the quest
for longevity or immortality, and liturgy and ritual (Palmer,
1991, p. 8).

One of the most important notions in Taoism is *wu-wei*,
the concept of non-action. According to Watts *wu* means
"not," and *wei* has a wide range of meanings, including
"action," "striving," "straining," and "doing." But perhaps
the best translation is "forcing," so "not forcing" is *wu-wei*. In
other words, "Tao accomplishes all things without forcing"
(1997, p. 8). Palmer (1991, p. 5) concurs: "In acting naturally,
by non-action, by just letting things be and following the
Way, the sage is in harmony with his own essence, the Tao
beyond unity. Being in harmony, he is in unity and all his
actions will thus express this unity and further it."

In this sense, the Tao is often likened to water: it does
not resist, yet nothing is stronger; it always takes the line
of least resistance, yet it always seeks the lowest level. The
lowest level is a "soft" position, yet it is the most powerful,
as can be seen in tai chi, judo, or aikido:

> In the arts of self-defense, you always get underneath
> the opponent, so he falls over you if he attacks you. The

moment he moves to be aggressive, you either go lower
than he is or move in a smaller circle than he is moving. So, the watercourse way is the way of Tao.[3] (Watts,
1997, p. 6)

In the Taoist view, because all beings and all other aspects
of the material world are fundamentally one, opposing opinions can only arise when people lose sight of the
"Whole" and regard their partial truths as absolute. They are
then like the frog at the bottom of the well who takes the bit
of brightness he sees for the whole sky. Thus, a Taoist sage
recognizes good and evil, true and false, but is neutral and
open to the extent that he offers no opposition to a would-
be opponent, whether it is a person or an idea: "When you
argue, there are some things you are failing to see. In the
greatest Tao nothing is named; in the greatest disputation,
nothing is said" (*Tao Te Ching*).

The quest for longevity or immortality, which is central to Taoist practices, involves two main approaches: (1)
introspection, meditation, and reflection, as illustrated in
the lifestyle of the reclusive sage; and (2) alchemy, or the
attempt to change the body physically into an eternal form
(Palmer, 1991).

Much of our knowledge of Taoism comes from the words
of ancient sages, such as Lao Tzu (the *Tao Te Ching*), Chuang
Tzu (his book is named after him), and Lieh Tzu (likewise).
In fact, the image of "the reclusive sage" who retires to a
mountain cave in order to meditate and reflect on life is very
powerful in Taoism, as the following verse illustrates (ibid.,
pp. 1 & 3):

In a back lane a sage quietly lived a simple life,
having just enough food to keep himself alive.
Poor and miserable though he might seem,
yet he felt happy and held himself in high esteem.

Much of Taoist practice is also concerned with the cultivation of the body's vital energy (ch'i) in an attempt to attain
refinement and longevity. The idea of immortality is central to Taoism, although this is not just a spiritual concept
and the physical body plays an important role: "immortality consists of transforming the whole body into an eternal
vehicle for the soul" (ibid., p. 1).

For the ancient Chinese, spirit and matter formed a con-
tinuum of vital energies, deriving from Heaven and Earth.
Techniques of longevity were developed to prevent the
scattering of these energies, which would result in death.
They also sought to refine the heavy, coarse energies of the
mundane world into something refined, light, and immor-
tal. Many Taoist physiological practices were influenced by
Indian Yoga, and the use of Chinese herbal medicine arose
from Taoist practice. In addition, the practice of acupuncture and tai chi both owe much to Taoist influence.

Finally, through the use of liturgy (i.e., forms of public
religious worship) and ritual, the Taoist seeks to become "a
channel or agent through which the world is kept in balance, evil forces are overcome, and life is continued and
improved—all through harnessing oneself to the forces of
the cosmos, the forces emanating from the Tao" (ibid., p. 10).

## TAOISM AND ZEN

There was never an attempt to implant Taoism officially
in Japan, although a random selection of Taoist beliefs and
customs have, at various times, been adopted and modified to the Japanese way of life. However, Taoist mysticism
greatly influenced the Chinese Ch'an (Zen) schools of Buddhism which were transplanted to Japan in the Kamakura
period.

In fact, Watts (1997, p. 82) claims that "Zen Buddhism … is
a Buddhist extension of Taoism [that] arose out of the mar-

riage of Buddhism and Taoism in the fifth century A.D. and over the following centuries": Taoism had a great "influence on the school of Mahayana Buddhism in China known as Ch'an Buddhism. Ch'an became Zen in Japan, and although in its Japanese form Zen became associated with the samurai, it retains to this day a Taoist flavor in its appreciation of the advantages of emptiness."

Thus, the ultimate synthesis of Taoism and Buddhism was realized in the Ch'an tradition, and in Japan, Zen soon became associated with the most important aspects of medieval Japanese culture.

## NOTES

1. The I Ching, or Book of Changes, is based on 64 unique six-line symbols known as hexagrams. There are two kinds of lines: solid Yang lines and broken Yin lines. These two types of lines can be grouped into a total of eight three-line figures, which are called trigrams, and which are an intermediate step in the formation of the final six-line hexagrams. The names of the trigrams are Heaven, Earth, Water, Fire, Wind, Mountain, Thunder, and Lake. These trigrams are then paired to form the hexagrams, and these 64 different pairings of the eight different trigrams represent the elements or forms of life. The quality of any given moment or situation can be represented by a hexagram generated during that moment or situation, since central to Taoist thought is the belief that the microcosm reflects the macrocosm (cf. Western astrology). These hexagrams can be used for divination purposes, as The Book of Changes provides an interpretation for each hexagram (Watts, 1997, pp. 33–34).

2. Taoism denies the validity of language, as the opening verse of the Tao Te Ching illustrates: "The Tao that can be spoken of is not the real Tao. The name that can be named

is not the true name." Because of this, the great books of Taoism, such as the *Tao Te Ching*, the *Chuang Tzu*, and the *Lieh Tzu*, use very cryptic terms and imagery. According to Palmer (1991, p. 7), "they are attempts to use both language and metaphor, whilst at the same time hinting that these are fundamentally inadequate."

3. According to Watts (1997, pp. 78–79), "judo ["the gentle way"] is a Japanese development of the Taoist philosophy, and it is relatively modern. But it comes out of understandings that emerged from Chinese ways of doing things, and in its present form it is a basic demonstration of the principle of *wu-wei*."

## DISCUSSION ACTIVITIES

1. Discuss the influences of Taoism on Japanese culture and belief systems. For example, the influence of Taoism can be found in the use of the Chinese calendar and in popular beliefs such as those concerning fortune-telling and auspicious directions. What are some other influences of Taoism in Japan?

2. What prevented Taoism from becoming institutionalized in Japan, in contrast to Buddhism and Confucianism?

3. According to the Taoist view of creation, all parts of the universe are attuned to a rhythmical pulsation, nothing is static, and all life is subject to periodic transformations. However, much of Taoist practice is concerned with an attempt to attain longevity. There is a contradiction between the notions "nothing is static" and "longevity." How can this be explained?

4. Discuss the influence of Taoism on Zen Buddhism. In addition, discuss the similarities and differences between Taoism and Zen.

5. Buddhists have temples, Shintoists have shrines, Christians have churches, and Muslims have mosques. Yet Taoists have no formal places of worship, nor any official community or center of authority. How can people identify themselves as Taoists? How can Taoism have survived for so long without any official community or center of authority? Discuss the relationship between religious community, center of authority, and religious belief.

6. Have you ever been involved in any activities related to Taoism, such as tai chi, acupuncture, or Chinese herbal medicine? What do you think about these practices.

7. In Japan, "teaching without words" can often be seen in the relationship between masters and disciples, especially during "*dō* lessons." On the other hand, there are manuals (*manuaru* or *terikisho*) for a great many situations, such as work-related practices, hobbies, and so forth. Explain this contradiction.

8. Many Japanese expressions contain the *kanji dō* (道), and these words reflect a wide range of meanings. The following are examples of the ways in which *dō* can be used in Japanese: *dōkyō*: Taoism; Shinto: "the way of the gods"; *dōro*: street or road; *dōjō*: practice room; *dōtoku*: morals; *dōraku*: entertainment; *bushidō*: "the way of the warrior"; *kadō*: flower arrangement (*ikebana*); *shodō*: calligraphy; *sadō*: tea ceremony; *kendō*: swordsmanship; *kyūdō*: archery; judo: "the soft way"; aikido: meeting/energy/way; and so forth. Why

are some of these words written in italics, while others are in roman print? What does this tell you about the "internationalization" of Japanese culture?

# Zen

## INTRODUCTION

After its adoption from China in the 6th century, Buddhism "permeated the whole intellectual, artistic, and social life of Japan" for well over a thousand years. It helped to transform the country from a primitive tribal region into a highly civilized nation-state, and in so doing, had a deep and lasting effect on both the spiritual and aesthetic values of the Japanese people (Reischauer, 1988). Claiborne notes that "so thoroughly integrated into the Japanese psyche have the assumptions and values of Buddhism become that their influence is apparent in every aspect of the lives of the people of modern Japan" (1993, p. 62). Lafcadio Hearn (1904, p. 225), the Irish-American chronicler of Japanese life at the turn of the century states:

> [Buddhism] educated the race, from the highest to the humblest, both in ethics and esthetics. All that can be classed under the name of art in Japan was either introduced or developed by Buddhism; and the same may be said regarding nearly all Japanese literature possessing real literary quality. . . . Buddhism introduced drama, the

higher forms of poetical composition, and fiction, and
history, and philosophy. All the refinements of Japanese
life were of Buddhist introduction. . . . Buddhism brought
the whole of Chinese civilization into Japan.

By far the most influential stream of Buddhist thought on
Japanese culture was Zen, which is perhaps best defined as
"the meditation school of East Asian Buddhism" (*Kodansha*,
1983, p. 370). However, Zen monks engaged not only in religious and meditative activities but also in diplomacy and
the cultural arts, including literature, painting, architecture,
gardening, and so forth.

## THE ORIGINS OF ZEN

Zen, in its original Chinese form of Ch'an Buddhism (Chinese Ch'an: from Sanskrit *dhyâna*, meaning meditation; the
Japanese pronunciation of the *kanji* for Ch'an is *zenno*), was
strongly influenced by indigenous Taoist thought. According to Snelling (1990, p. 98), "Zen is really a Chinese development, incorporating elements of the indigenous traditions,
notably Taoism."

The founder of the Ch'an school was the Indian monk
Bodhidharma, who brought his teachings on meditation in
the lotus posture culminating in sudden realization to China
around 520 AD. By the time it reached Japan, Chinese Zen
"had reached a certain plateau in its development," and the
type of meditation it espoused had "taken on a definitive
form and was practiced seriously and successfully" (ibid.).

The introduction of the Ch'an school into Japan from
China is "one of the most important events in Japanese
religious history" (ibid.). Zen was introduced into Japan
c. 1200 AD by the Buddhist monk Eisai, who founded the
Rinzai sect, known for its strict meditation system and use
of *kōan* riddles (Chinese: *kung-an*), or enigmatic, paradoxi-

Zen Pebble and Rake

cal, non-logical statements used with novices "to exhaust their thinking and thereby progress in meditation" (e.g., "What is the sound of one hand clapping?") (ibid.).[1] Another form of Zen, the Soto sect, was later founded by Dogen, a disciple of Eisai. Soto Zen also made meditation its essential practice, but rejected the *kōan*. It emphasized *zazen* (*za*: sitting; *zen*: meditation; from the Chinese *zuochan*), or silent sitting and meditating on whatever illumination or insight is received while waiting in silence[2] (see Appendix H). Taking advantage of increasing cultural exchanges between Japan and China, Eisai and Dogen, as well as many other Japanese Buddhist monks, studied at Ch'an schools in China and thereafter worked tirelessly to propagate their tenets in Japan (ibid.).

Zen quickly became established in Japan, and Zen temples were built throughout the country, becoming "active cultural centers as well as sites of religious practice" (ibid.). By means of these provincial temples, Zen had a great impact on the people, and during this period it exerted a formative influence on the arts of ink painting (sumi-e), Noh drama, the tea ceremony, flower arrangement, landscaping, and so forth. "The aesthetics nurtured in these arts was to remain a definitive force in Japanese culture during the following centuries" (ibid.).[3]

Because it taught such a direct and unhesitating way of life, Zen also had a strong impact on the martial arts and the military class in Japan (bushidō, or "the way of the warrior," is thought to be a combination of Zen training and Confucian loyalty). Since samurai were also extensively trained in scholarship and the arts, Zen became one of the most important influences on the cultural and aesthetic expression of the Japanese people. Zen also stipulated that its practitioners should defend the Japanese state, and could observe ceremonial rules and offer prayers, both necessary conditions for its appeal to the warrior class.[4]

Zen Garden
Stepping
Stones

## ZEN BELIEFS

Zen stresses that the Buddha-nature (cf. Tao) resides in all things, but that this reality cannot not be taught because it is beyond duality and conceptualization. In Zen, as in Taoism, essential truth is incommunicable—enlightenment (*satori*) is sought in immediate experience and spiritual peace and the Absolute is found in the phenomenal world. Zen emphasizes that all human beings originally possess the Buddha-nature within themselves and need only the actual experience of it to achieve enlightenment. Enlightenment is seen as a liberation from man's intellectual nature, from the burden of fixed ideas and feelings about reality— "Zen always aims at grasping the central fact of life, which can never be brought to the dissecting table of the intellect" (Suzuki, 1964, p. 51). Those who are enlightened cannot explain this ultimate truth, which is both radically simple and self-evident but beyond the ordinary duality of subject and object. It cannot be conveyed by books, words, concepts, or teachers, but must be realized by immediate and direct personal experience.

Zen is neither a religion nor a philosophy, but rather a contemplative form of mysticism which disdains study, reason, and metaphysics, and stresses the flash of intuition obtained in meditation. Like other forms of Buddhism, it is loosely organized and lacking in any strongly defined principle of authority. Although Zen reveres the historical Buddha, training and practice is focused in the person of the Master, as it is believed that instruction from a Master can awaken in a disciple the Buddha-nature that everyone possesses:

> Enlightenment means seeing your own essential nature and this at the same time means seeing through to the essential nature of the cosmos and of all things. For seeing through to essential nature is the window to enlight-

enment. One may call essential nature truth if one wants
to. In Buddhism from ancient times it has been called . . .
Buddha-nature or one Mind. In Zen it has been called
nothingness. . . . The designations may be different, but
the content is completely the same. (Zen master Hakūun
Yasutani Roshi; as cited in Scott & Doubleday, 1992, p. 2)

## ZEN PRACTICES

The unique contribution of Zen has been the many methods
of reaching and presenting the truth that have been used by
Zen masters. Based on the *mondō*, or brief dialogues between
Master and disciple, Zen's peculiar method of instruction
entails simply pointing to the truth, the "real now," without
interposing ideas and notions about it. For the Zen Master,
the best way to express one's deepest experiences is by the
use of paradoxes which transcend opposites (e.g., "Where
there is nothing, there is all" or "To die the great death is to
gain the great life."). These sayings illustrate two irreducible
Zen dilemmas—the inexpressibility of truth in words, and
that "opposites are relational and so fundamentally harmo-
nious" (Watts, 1957, p. 175).

Zen training stresses both stillness and action, and these
are expressed through the disciplines of meditation and
daily work (unlike some other forms of Buddhism, all Zen
schools are self-sufficient—"The monk who does not work
will not eat."). In Zen, it is thought that the Buddha-nature
dwells hidden in all of the inconspicuous things of daily
life, and that the harmony of mind and body is "achiev-
able through the simultaneous stilling of one's mind and
purposeful activation of the organs of physical perception"
(Claiborne, 1993, p. 76).

In all forms of activity, Zen emphasizes the importance
of acting naturally, gracefully, and spontaneously in whatever task one is performing, an attitude that has greatly

Zen Monks Ninnaji Temple

influenced all forms of cultural expression in Japan. The single-mindedness of Japanese martial and aesthetic arts, for example, illustrates the Zen principles of detachment and equanimity, the expanded consciousness beyond the "me-state" in which each moment flows unimpeded by one's awareness of anything except the alert yet relaxed stance of the swordsman or the ritual movements of the making of tea (ibid., p. 69). Suzuki (1964, p. 51) suggests that the total attentiveness of Zen thus incorporates the principles of emptiness, nothingness, quietude, and no-thought.

## ZEN AND JAPANESE CULTURE

An important Zen teaching that has profound implications for the communicative style of the Japanese is that intellectually contrived distinctions are limiting, and that language, as the primary instrument of intellectuality, therefore interferes with true understanding. From the Zen standpoint, "the world as it is viewed from the dualistic perspective is a necessary but artificial construct generated by the activity of thought moving through the medium of language" (Claiborne, 1993, p. 65). Linguistic forms are thus thought to be distracting echoes of the mind at play—in Zen, wisdom and eloquence are found in silence, rather than in the verbalization of human conceptualizations—"by stillness, as well as in action, one discovers knowledge" (ibid., p. 62). As Claiborne (ibid., p. 72) notes, this privileging of silence over words, the implicit over the explicit, as well as a distrust in the power of analytical reasoning except for certain purposes has strongly influenced Japanese consciousness and all forms of resulting cultural expression.

The Zen emphasis on the immediate, intuitive experience of truth and on its direct transmission from teacher to disciple has also had a profound effect on Japanese aesthetic expression. Zen, and its community of wandering monks, became associated with the most important facets of medieval Japanese art and literature,[5] infusing them with its spirit—the belief in the ineffability of mystical experience, the tenet that all metaphysical views are only partial apprehensions of the whole truth (which lies beyond rational analysis), the assumption that only by detaching oneself from philosophical oppositions can one apprehend the truth.

All the Zen arts "breathe the spirit of Zen" and are called "ways" (*dō*; cf. Tao), "whether painting, landscaping, tea ceremony, calligraphy, and poetics fostered in the temples, or the military skills of archery, swordsmanship, and martial arts practiced in the wider sphere of the temples' influence" (*Kodansha*, 1983, p. 374). The practice of any of these aesthetic or martial arts can also lead to a genuine Zen experience. "Simplicity, naturalness, harmony, precision—in short, the essentials of action and achievement—are the hallmarks of the spirit of Zen" (ibid.).

## NOTES

1. A *kōan* cannot be solved rationally. "The practitioner is obliged to 'hold' the *kōan* constantly in mind, day and night. Concentration increases until the tension causes rational thinking to give way under the pressure and a breakthrough occurs," opening the door to a new way of seeing (*Kodansha*, 1983, p. 373).

2. *Zazen* is not entirely of Zen origin, since the basic form was taken from traditional Indian yoga; e.g., sitting in the lotus position during meditation (ibid.).

3. The aesthetic principles that developed around Zen became "a lasting element of Japanese culture" (see Appendix I):

The small, the simple, the natural, even the misshapen were valued over the large, the grandiose, the artificial, or the uniform. In architecture, natural wood textures . . . were preferred. Small gardens were designed to represent in microcosm the wild grandeur of nature. . . . In painting, a few bold, expert strokes of black India ink caught . . . the essence of nature. . . . The tea ceremony was developed as an esthetic cult, gracefully performed in simple surroundings and with simple utensils. This medieval Zen esthetic was well suited to the austere life of feudal Japan. . . . (Reischauer, 1988, pp. 62–63)

4. The samurai saw in the concepts of simplicity and closeness to nature, as well as the rigorous self-discipline of Zen meditation, "a way to develop the self-control and firmness of character their way of life demanded" (ibid., pp. 61–62).

5. Zen monks were advisers to the Shoguns, and through their influence there was "a great resurgence of interest in Chinese scholarship and literature and a revival of skill in the writing of the Chinese language." From China, they also imported landscape painting, gardening, and tea drinking (to keep the meditator awake) (ibid., p. 62).

## DISCUSSION ACTIVITIES

1. Scholars are still debating the relationship between Zen and Taoism. There are two points of view in this debate: one that "Zen is a form of Buddhism"; the other is that "Zen is a form of Taoism." Although there is no doubt that Zen monks in Japan have always considered themselves to be Buddhists, there are many aspects of Zen which derive directly from Taoism. For example, some authors use the term "Zen Buddhism," while others use the term "Zen." Which point of view do you think is more accurate?

2. It is said that all of the aesthetic and martial arts of Japan are infused with "the spirit of Zen." Discuss what this means.

3. Have you ever tried to practice *zazen*? What effects did it have on you during and after the practice?

4. What is the Buddha-nature? How can we find it within ourselves?

5. Zen, which emphasizes meditation and silence, has strongly affected the Japanese people's way of life. However, this appears to be the opposite of today's loud, noisy, fast-paced Japan. How do you explain this?

6. The traditional Japanese diet (*shōjin ryōri*) originated in Zen monasteries of the Kamakura period. Describe this diet, its advantages, and its place in modern Japan.

7. In Zen, wisdom and eloquence are found in silence. In Japan, those who speak eloquently are sometimes disdained and not trusted, and those who like arguments are occasionally considered immature. Does this have something to do with the fact that the Japanese people tend to avoid discussion and debate and sometimes have difficulty in developing effective communication skills? Should they practice more verbal expression and analytical reasoning in schools?

8. It is sometimes said that Japan's greatest contribution to world culture is Zen Buddhism. Yet of all the forms of Buddhism, Zen is one of the least commonly followed in Japan today, while it is among the most commonly studied and practiced in the West? Why do so few Japanese people seem to be interested in Zen today?

9. In Europe and North America, there are many Zen monasteries where the disciplines of meditation and daily work (i.e., both the stillness and action that Zen training stresses) are practiced. Zen seems to be quite popular in Western countries. How do people in the West perceive Zen and why are they attracted to it?

10. Zen Buddhism has had a very important influence on many practices in Japan, emphasizing self-discipline and the Zen spirit in all forms of activity. Give examples of Zen training that still exist in daily Japanese life.

11. It is said that Japanese martial arts involve both spiritual refinement and technical practice. What about the aesthetic arts, such as *shodō*, *sadō*, or *kadō*?

12. Discuss the origins of Zen. Where did it come from? How did it develop? Why did it come to be so important in Japanese culture?

# Confucianism

## INTRODUCTION

If Taoism is concerned with the ultimate unity of man and the cosmos, Confucianism emphasizes human society and the social responsibilities of its members. Thus, the two traditions, "beyond society" and "within society," balance and complement one another in the Chinese tradition, and although they are considered to be two distinct belief systems today, at one time they were probably two parts of the same whole in Chinese religious and philosophical thought.

Confucianism is primarily a code of ethics and system of philosophy and not a religion in the true sense of the word. There is no concept of deity, and although there are revered texts, there is no worship, no priesthood, and no emphasis on metaphysics. There is "only right thinking and right living, as shown particularly through loyalty to the ruler, filial piety to one's father, and strict observance of proper social ritual and etiquette" (Reischauer, 1988, p. 203). Watts (1995, p. 92) concurs, stating that Confucianism is essentially "a social ritual and a way of ordering society."

## THE ORIGINS OF CONFUCIANISM

East Asians call Confucianism the school of *ju* (or "the teach-ing of the scholars"; cf. Japanese *jukyō*), but in the West it was named for its first master, Confucius (Latinized from the Chinese, K'ung-fu-tzu; cf. Koshi in Japanese), who lived around 550 BC and was said to have been a contemporary of Lao-tzu, the founder of the Taoist way (Watts, 1995, p. 91). Classical Confucianism became the official philosophy of the Han Dynasty (202 BC–220 AD), where it helped to shape the social and political institutions of ancient China, later spreading to other East Asian countries where it had a far-reaching impact through its rich literary legacy of ethi-cal teachings, political lore, history, poetry, and ritual texts (Sansom, 1976).

Neo-Confucianism was a revitalized form of Confu-cianist thought that originated in Sung Dynasty China in the 12th century at a time when Buddhism had fallen into decline. The major feature of society in this period was the emergence of a bureaucratic and cultural elite, as well as an emphasis on civil as opposed to military rule, which encour-aged scholarship and secular education. As a result, there was an expansion of civil service examinations for a rapidly growing number of bureaucrats, and a heightened demand for education at all levels. The model for the education of state officials became a combination of Confucian study and practical learning, such as civil administration, engineering, and mathematics. The study of the Confucian Classics was considered important in providing values and principles for ordering and structuring the newly available practical knowledge (ibid.).

The Five Classics, as well as a selection of related second-ary texts, still constitute the common literary heritage of all educated Chinese, who know many of the outstanding passages by heart. The subjects of the Classics are diverse—divination, ritual forms, ancient poetry, historical records, the teachings of Confucius, and so forth. They were written in a formal classical style of extreme brevity and compactness, in which single written characters had a wide range of meanings. As a result, many interpretations were needed, and for centuries scholars provided commentaries on the Classics that are often more lengthy than the texts themselves.

This form of scholarship became the norm for government, law, schooling, literary composition, and human behavior in China for 2,000 years, and eventually became the most dominant social and political force in all of East Asia, where it became institutionalized in the formal curricula of educational systems and in civil service exams for government officials in Korea and Japan as well.[1]

## CONFUCIAN VALUES

Confucianism is first and foremost a rational, utilitarian philosophy of human nature which considers proper human relationships as the basis of society. In both its classical and later forms, Confucianism stresses a social order based on strict ethical rules, centering on the family and state, both of which should be governed by men of education and superior ethical wisdom.

Confucianism emphasizes right thinking, right living, and the strict observance of proper social etiquette, as set down in four principles of right conduct:

(1) *jen*: humanism, the warm human feelings between people, the seed from which springs all the qualities of the ideal human being, related in daily practice to the concept of reciprocity (trying to understand how it would feel to be the other person, to empathize with others)

(2)  i: faithfulness, loyalty, or justice (the opposite of individ-
     ual interest and profit)

(3)  li: propriety, ritual, respect for social forms, decorum
     (the fundamental regulatory etiquette of human behav-
     ior which follows from jen, from being considerate of
     others)

(4)  chih: wisdom (as well as a liberal education)

The central values of Confucianism thus stress both the
education of the noble man and ritual order within the family as the embodiment of the ideal community. In Confucian society, the family stands at the centre and serves as a
bridge between the individual and the state, and the properly cultivated man is educated in preparation for regulating
the family, then the state itself. In this way, the ideal for the
individual man is "sageness within, kingliness without," as
embodied in the founding myth of the sage-king, Yao, who
was a perfect personification of wisdom, dignity, and self-
restraint, illustrating the Confucian concept of leadership by
the wise and the worthy.[2]


## CONFUCIANISM IN JAPAN

Confucianism, in both its classical and later forms, can be
considered a further layer in the Japanese belief system. It
was imported into Japan during three successive historical periods and played a much different role in Japanese life
than either Shinto or Buddhism.

Elements of classical Confucianism initially entered
Japan with many other aspects of Chinese civilization in the
first great wave of influence that resulted from the wholesale adoption of Buddhist practices from the 6th to the 9th
centuries. When the Chinese writing system was introduced

to Japan, much of its Confucian content came with it, and Confucian ethics, political institutions, and educational values were thus inseparably linked with the study of the Chinese language.

At first, Confucianism was overshadowed by Buddhist beliefs and practices, and as a result its greatest impact was not felt until much later, starting with a second wave of influence in the form of Neo-Confucianism in medieval times. During this period, from the 12th to the 17th centuries, Confucian learning became the sole ingredient of an intellectual education in Japan, and was spread throughout the country by Zen Buddhist monks.

The emergence of the Tokugawa shogunate in the 17th century, with its emphasis on law and order, unquestioning obedience, and governmental control of the populace, marked the beginning of a third period of influence. Neo-Confucianism gradually replaced Buddhism, and Confucian schools of philosophy dominated Japanese thought. Confucian values and ethics were institutionalized at all levels of Japanese social and political life during the Edo period, until by the 19th century "the Japanese had become as thoroughly Confucian as their Chinese and Korean counterparts, despite their very non-Confucian feudal political system" (Reischauer, 1988, p. 204).[3]

When Japan came into contact with these Confucian ideals, there was little resistance from indigenous social patterns and ways of thinking, since the two value systems suited one another remarkably in a number of important ways. Confucianism's rational and practical social philosophy was very much in keeping with the secular orientation of the Japanese, and its lack of metaphysical emphasis coincided well with the phenomenalist approach to life in Japan (Nakamura, 1971, p. 407 ff.).

Confucianism's concern with social conduct within a concrete human nexus also fit well with the dominant value system in Japan which placed primary importance on particularistic human relationships within a strictly-defined social hierarchy (ibid.). Filial piety, respect for one's elders, and reverence for one's ancestors also suited native Japanese preferences. The present-day emphasis in Japanese life on education, diligence, and historical precedent (i.e., accumulated knowledge from the past as opposed to intellectual debate) all owe much to Confucian influences.

Nevertheless, as with other imported traditions, the Japanese adopted Confucian ideals and institutions selectively; thus, "loyalty" in the Confucian sense became synonymous with loyalty to the emperor, and civil service exams, although widely implemented, were restricted to the aristocracy. Confucianism was, however, able to co-exist relatively easily with Shinto and Buddhism, illustrating once again the Japanese preference for synthesis and consensus formation rather than the assertion of one belief system over another (Sansom, 1976).

Confucianism did not survive the modernization of Japan in the late 19th century, as the Meiji government abandoned the old Confucian academies and instituted a Western system of education which emphasized scientific and technical learning. However, Confucian ethical values continue to permeate the thinking of modern Japanese, and according to Reischauer, perhaps with more influence than any of the other religious and philosophical traditions that have shaped Japanese culture:[4]

> Behind the wholehearted Japanese acceptance of modern science, modern concepts of growth and progress, universalistic principles of ethics, and democratic ideals and values, strong Confucian traits persist, such as the belief in the moral basis of government, the emphasis on interpersonal relationships and loyalties, and faith in education and hard work. Almost no one considers him-

self a Confucianist today, but in a sense almost all Japanese are. (1988, p. 204)

## NOTES

1. According to Fister-Stoga (1993, p. 143), Chinese verse typically contains four couplets designated metaphorically as "head, chin, neck, tail." This pattern is evident in the traditional essay form, the *ba gu*, or "eight-legged essay," which was "one of the central genres in the Chinese civil service examination from the fourteenth to the twentieth century," and first employed by the Japanese in the Edo era. The content of the *ba gu* dealt with the Confucian classics and its structure was rigidly prescribed, even to the point of the number of characters allowed. The first section of the essay introduces the theme, the second section develops it, the third section, or "turn," views the theme from a different angle, and the fourth section sets forth a conclusion (ibid., p. 144). "Since each of the four sections had to contain a *parallel* structure within itself, the form was considered to have 'eight legs'" (ibid.). The discourse type known as *ki-shō-ten-ketsu*, which still plays a central role in Japanese rhetoric and composition pedagogy, follows a similar pattern and was originally taken from a form of classical Chinese poetry known as *qi-cheng-zhuan-he* (起承転合) (ibid., p. 143). Of interest here is the fact that "the *qi-cheng-zhuan-he* pattern [also] appears in one of the preferred Korean rhetorical patterns, the *ki-sung-chon-kyul*" (ibid.), which is still used extensively today in Korea (Eggington, 1987). Thus, the *ki-shō-ten-ketsu*, like the *ki-sung-chon-kyul*, is an imported pattern from China, adopted into Japan due to the immense prestige of classical Chinese culture (Fister-Stoga, 1993, p. 145).

2. Watts (1995, p. 93) claims that Confucianism has been one of the most successful philosophies in all of history for

the regulation of relationships within government and the family: "Confucianism prescribes all kinds of formal relationships—linguistic, ceremonial, musical, in etiquette, and in all the spheres of the morals."

3. Confucian texts were brought to Japan by the Korean envoy and scholar Wani in the fifth century AD, some 900 years after the death of Confucius (Buddhist sutras were also among the gifts). According to Hoffman (2006, p. 7), "Japan's cultural and political infancy, then, bears a strong Confucian stamp. A Chinese visitor to Nara at the height of the Nara period would have seen a model in miniature of his own society." Although the Heian period witnessed a waning of interest in Confucianism, the close of this period "coincided with a Chinese recasting of the Confucian legacy by a group of scholars known to posterity as neo-Confucianists. The outstanding figure among them as far as Japan is concerned is Chu Hsi" (ibid.; cf. *shushigaku*, or "Chu Hsi School"). His thinking was attractive to the ultraconservative regime of the Edo period, when "the Tokugawa shoguns closed Japan to all but the most limited foreign intercourse and froze, to the greatest extent possible, the social system in its 17th-century mold. Throughout this period, Chu Hsi's neo-Confucianism was the official state dogma" (ibid.).

4. In fact, "the world's tallest statue of Confucius, standing 4.57 meters high, graces the grounds of Yushima Seido in Ochanomizu, Tokyo. Yushima Seido is a 17th century Confucian temple [where] students congregate . . . in droves to pray for success in their examinations" (ibid.).

## DISCUSSION ACTIVITIES

1. Some scholars maintain that Confucianism is not a religion, but is closer to a form of philosophy. In other words,

in Confucianism there is no concept of deity, and although there are revered texts, there is no worship, no priesthood, and no emphasis on metaphysics. Why then did it become as influential as Shinto and Buddhism in Japan?

2. Confucian ethical values continue to permeate the thinking of modern Japanese, and according to some scholars, with more influence than any of the other religious and philosophical traditions that have shaped Japanese culture. Where do you see the influences of Confucianism in Japan?

3. Confucianism stresses a social order based on strict ethical rules and proper human relationships, centered on the family and state, both of which should be governed by men of education and superior wisdom. What exactly are these strict rules and proper human relationships? What are their advantages and disadvantages for modern societies?

4. Japan's "ie ideology" arose from a hierarchical system of family membership which originated in the pre-modern period and which is still dominant in Japanese consciousness. Discuss the influence of Confucianism on the ie system.

5. What is the difference between Classical Confucianism and Neo-Confucianism? Discuss how they were both accepted in Japan ?

6. Confucianism regards both respect for the elderly and ancestor worship as important. Why should people follow these ideas today?

7. Although the Meiji government abandoned the Confucian academies of the Tokugawa era, Confucianism helped the rapid modernization of Japan with its principles of rational and practical ways of thinking and its sense of the impor-

tance of diligence. Compare education in modern and pre-modern Japan.

8. The Japanese have long tended to put group interests before personal ones, but this tendency became even stronger after Confucian values were introduced from China. Discuss this trait in terms of Japanese people's sense of belonging to their companies or other organizations?

9. Contemporary Japanese tend to have a negative image of Confucianism. Why?

10. Confucianism had a great influence on the feudal political system during the Tokugawa shogunate, at which time samurai families existed within a hereditary framework that was based on loyalty to the Shogun. Many Japanese politicians nowadays also seem to have created hereditary systems. Do you think this is due to Confucian influences?

11. Many Confucian values are admirable, particularly those related to filial piety, loyalty, and humility. However, Confucianism was also responsible for controlling ordinary people through a sense of hierarchy, and women, especially, were traditionally excluded from centers of power in Confucian societies. Discuss these issues in terms of the place of women in modern Japan.

12. There is often a danger in generalizing specific cultural patterns to large geographical areas. Do you think that China, Korea, and Japan should be grouped together in East Asia as being strongly affected by Confucianism? Where and how can the influence of Confucianism be seen in East Asia? What are some of the differences among East Asian countries in terms of this Confucian influence?

13. There is a saying in Japanese: "Stay three paces behind to avoid stepping on your master's shadow." The word "master" originally meant teacher, but came to mean any of one's superiors. It is said that women were supposed to walk three paces behind their husbands in the past in Japan, perhaps because a wife's position was considered secondary to her husband's. Compare this idea with the concept "ladies first" in Western chivalry.

14. A culture that is influenced by Confucian beliefs holds that a healthy family unit is fundamental to the creation of an ethical civilization because the ethical values of the family affect the functioning of society as a whole. In this family unit, Confucianism overwhelmingly emphasizes the superiority of males in a leadership role; i.e., "the properly cultivated man." Contemporary Japan continues to be a thoroughly male-dominated society; however, the governance of the family is done mostly with an absent father and household responsibilities are almost always left in the hands of the mother. Has this anomaly always existed in Japan, and how can this discrepancy be reconciled in a nation so heavily steeped in Confucian traditions?

# Western Influences in the Modern Era

## BACKGROUND

The political reunification of Japan, which marked the beginning of the Edo period after centuries of almost constant civil conflict (*sengoku jidai*), was accomplished by a succession of military leaders, the last of whom was Tokugawa Ieyasu. At the beginning of the 17th century, he closed Japan to the outside world (*sakoku*, or closed-nation policy), and moved the capital from Kyoto to his power base in eastern Japan at Edo (Tokyo), where his central administration developed into a large bureaucracy. His heirs remained rulers of Japan until the middle of the 19th century, assuming the old title of Shogun. These two centuries were ones of relative peace for Japan which "permitted the Japanese to work over and perfect their own rich cultural heritage. During this period they became culturally more homogenous and developed an extremely strong sense of national identity" (Reischauer, 1988, p. 68).

During the Edo period, society was divided strictly into four classes (*shi-nō-kō-shō*): the warrior rulers (*bushi*); the peasants, who were basically farmers (*nōgyo*); the artisans and craftsmen (*kōgyo*); and at the bottom, the merchants (*shōgyo*). The Tokugawa government valued agriculture and taxed it heavily, but taxed trade only lightly and indirectly. This led to the growth of a prosperous urban merchant class and the development of great merchant houses in such fields as sake brewing, retailing dry goods, and money lending.

The samurai class also underwent great changes at this time. Constituting about 6% of the total population, it was transformed from a fighting force to a hereditary civil bureaucracy, and samurai became men of the writing brush rather than the sword. Virtually the whole of the samurai class became literate, as did the merchants and wealthier peasants, and people started to delve more deeply into neo-Confucian scholarship.

Isolation, such as that which occurred in Japan during this time is usually associated with cultural stagnation, but the long peace and economic stability of the Edo period led instead to "a veritable cultural explosion" (ibid.). There was a great increase in the number of Confucian academies, men in touch with the Dutch traders in Nagasaki studied medicine, metallurgy, and gunnery ("Dutch learning"), and there was development in all forms of the arts. In particular, because of the rise of an urban merchant culture, in the amusement quarters of the cities, new types of art, theater, and literature, distinct from those cultivated by the samurai, started to evolve, and were known as *ukiyo-e*, or "pictures of the fleeting world."[1] Art forms that arose from this fertile cultural milieu included *Yamato-e* paintings, *kabuki* dramas, and haiku poetry. Hence, "while the general political pattern remained rigidly unchanging, beneath the surface there were great dynamic tensions between Confucian and feudal values, and between economic growth and a frozen class society" (ibid., p. 77).

Despite these tensions, the Tokugawa regime would have lasted much longer except that rapid advances in technology in the West no longer made this possible. Industrialization was bringing Western economic and military power to the shores of Japan, and the pressures were more than the Tokugawa system could sustain. In 1853, Japan was reluctantly forced to give American ships access to its ports by Commodore Perry, and shortly thereafter the whole antiquated structure of the Tokugawa government began to disintegrate.

This breakdown took some 15 years to reach its conclusion, but in 1868 a group of young reformers in the samurai ranks led a short uprising which resulted in the reinstatement of imperial rule by the emperor, whose family had been living quietly and without real power in Kyoto during the previous two centuries. These reformers took the West as their model, changing the old motto of "expel the barbarians" to the new slogan of "rich country, strong military" (*fukoku kyohei*) (ibid., p. 81). The country was opened up and the Westerners themselves were used to bring about reforms. However, replacing the old feudal system with a more effective centralized rule and starting the technological modernization of Japan was an immense task. The country was burdened with a "broken-down, bankrupt shogunal domain, . . . divided into autonomous feudal units and still limited to a purely preindustrial economy" (ibid.).

The government was modernized largely on the model of the 19th century West, and ministries like those in European countries were formed. These included a Finance Ministry, which oversaw the development of a modern banking system and reform of the monetary system with the yen as its unit. The Army and Navy Ministries were based on the German model, while a modern court and legal system, modeled on French and German systems, was in place by 1899. In addition, an infrastructure of railroads, port facilities, and a telegraph network was developed. To achieve these goals, a great deal of Western technical expertise was needed, so the government dispatched students abroad to acquire new skills and hired Western experts at great expense to come to Japan.

Reforms of the education system at this time are particularly instructive since education played such a significant role in the modernization of Japan from both positive and negative perspectives. Because of the traditional emphasis on learning in Japan,[2] it was not difficult for the Meiji reformers to understand that education was going to be a key to their success. In 1871, a Ministry of Education was established based on the French model and designed for a highly centralized and uniform school system (at this time about 45% of males and 15% of females were literate). None of the *terakoya* (Buddhist village schools) or Confucian academies survived the transition to the Western style of wholly secular and egalitarian education. The Japanese placed "their chief emphasis on elementary education, thus laying a firm foundation both for the nation and for higher education" (ibid., pp. 187–188).[3] At the top of the educational pyramid was Tokyo University which was established in 1877 as an amalgam of three shogunal schools: a Confucian academy (later dropped), a school of medicine, and a school of foreign learning. The government created new imperial universities one after another: Kyoto in 1897, Tohoku in 1907, and so forth. In 1918, a number of private schools were granted university status, the most prestigious of which are Keio and Waseda. Even today, the great majority of Japan's leaders come from a small group of these prestigious universities.[4]

As Reischauer (ibid., p. 85) points out, when the history of Japan from the 1850s to the 1880s is examined, it stands out as a truly extraordinary experience. No other country in the world responded as "quickly and successfully to the challenge of superior Western economic and military technology." The reasons for this success can be attributed to a number of characteristics of the Japanese people, including their homogeneity and strong self-identity, as well as their clear awareness of the importance of learning from abroad due to their long association with China.

A new saying, which exemplified the philosophy of the times, was coined by the reformers who successfully transformed Japan: "Japanese culture for the basic conduct of life and Western knowledge for dealing with practical affairs"— in other words, "Western science and Eastern ethics"—and this approach still holds in Japan in many ways today. However, people soon realized that there was "no clear dividing line between techniques, institutions, and values. They tended to be all of a piece" (ibid., p. 129). As a result, it is difficult today to separate Western influences from the other layers of Japanese culture, so deeply have they become absorbed into Japanese life, and although most Japanese still maintain a rigid "us vs. them" worldview with regard to other peoples, the nation itself clearly has "a foot in both worlds," straddling East and West.

Although many of the events of these times are still too close and too controversial to be judged with the impartiality of history, and are difficult to analyze without adequate distance, from the standpoint of the underlying theme of this book, three elements stand out in terms of the influence of the West on the religious and philosophical foundations of Japanese culture in the modern era: State Shinto, Christianity, and secularism.

## STATE SHINTO

The modern Meiji state originated in response to external threats from the West, and as outlined above, it was based on the rapid assimilation of the institutions of the Western imperial powers. Pyle (2007, p. 75) notes that "the Japanese alone among Asian peoples accommodated quickly to the norms, principles and mores of the imperialist system" when first confronted by Western technological superiority. However, "it was a dangerous and rapacious world . . . that Japan [was] forced to join. . . . The strong devoured the weak and contended with one another for strategic advantages. Military strength appeared to the Japanese as essential as industrial power to win security and full independence" (Reischauer & Jansen, 1995, p. 348). In order to accomplish the goals of modernization, the Meiji government replaced the "hereditary social hierarchy [of the Edo era] with a merit-based competitive ethic, nationalism centered on the institution of the emperor, and state-engineered "thought guidance" of the population" (Pyle, op. cit.). Their two main vehicles for achieving these goals were State Shinto and the education system.

State Shinto (*Kokka Shinto*) was a creation of the Meiji government, which believed that Shinto could become a unifying agent to center the country around the Emperor by developing a strong sense of national unity and cultural identity among the people while the process of modernization was undertaken. It was also "a ruthless attack . . . on Buddhism as an element of the discredited past that stood in the way of the creation of an emperor centered new political system" (Reischauer & Jansen, 1995, p. 206). In this system, the emperor was worshipped as a living god (*akitsumikami*) as a central element in the new ideology for a rapidly modernizing Japan.

In pushing this agenda, one of the first acts of the Meiji government was to establish the Shinto Worship Bureau, which was designed to oversee religious affairs and administer the separation of Buddhism from Shinto. In 1871, all Shinto shrines in Japan became property of the central government, and all citizens were forced to register at their local shrine (in contrast to the Edo era in which families were required to register with Buddhist temples). In 1872, an Office of Shinto Worship was created to promote government-sponsored rites of worship, and all Shinto priests became civil servants (in other words, the state became merged with the new religion).[5] Later, prior to and during World War II, the government used State Shinto to encourage patriotism and support efforts towards nationalism and militarism. Citizens participated in public rituals modeled on ancient ceremonies in order to foster a sense of sacred duty in supporting the war effort (Breen, 2000; Hall, 1971).

Of particular interest is the way in which schools and state-engineered "guidance" bureaus were used to promote State Shinto, patriotism, and nationalism at this time. In 1890, the Imperial Rescript on Education proclaimed that all Japanese students were required to recite an oath in which they offered themselves to the State and to the Imperial family. The practice of emperor worship was further spread by having imperial portraits with the emperor dressed as the high priest of State Shinto in schools. Eventually, miniature Shinto shrines were built in school playgrounds throughout the country, and students were expected to worship at them daily. These practices were used to develop national solidarity through patriotic centralized observances at the shrines.

In fact, "education was to play a crucial role in effecting the state control of thought, both within and outside schools. According to Okano and Tsuchiya (1999, p. 24), "the government effectively used schooling as a political means to mobilise the people for the military expansion of its territory into Asia, [as well as for] the horrific oppression of its own people within the country." In consolidating the imperial ideology through education, a Bureau of Thought was created in the Ministry of Education in 1934, and later, military drills were adopted by many schools, while "a vigorous dissemination of the imperial ideology was conducted through school education and adult education groups." In

1940, indoctrination took even more intensified forms, with the military intervening in designing school curricula, the placement of ex-army officers in schools, and the making of military drills compulsory at all schools (ibid.).

Meanwhile, with the enactment of the Peace Preservation Law in 1925, a "Thought Police" section was formed within the Home Ministry, with branches all over Japan and in overseas locations with high concentrations of Japanese subjects in order to monitor activities by dissenters. A Student Section was also established under the Ministry of Education to monitor university professors and students, as part of the Ministry's Ideology Bureau. Within the Ministry of Justice, special "Thought Prosecutors" were appointed to prosecute the "thought criminals." In 1941, the Peace Preservation Law was completely re-written, with even more severe sanctions for people suspected of opposing the government. At this time, religious organizations were also placed under the authority of the Thought Police for the first time (Breen, 2000; Hall, 1971). University professors were pressured to recant and revise their books if they differed with imperial ideology (e.g., denying that the emperor was a living god), and universities were expected to dismiss faculty members who did not obey official guidelines. Between 1925 and 1945, over 70,000 people were arrested under the provisions of the Peace Preservation Law ("Thought Control Uncovered," 2006, p. 27).

This tragic period in Japanese history came to an end with the country's defeat in World War II, when the emperor issued a statement in which he announced that he was not an *akitsumikami*. The Allied Powers ordered the separation of the government from religious affairs, and the separation of church and state was later incorporated into the Japanese Constitution.

State Shinto was, in the end, a political expediency, "a phantom concoction of the Meiji government" in its attempt to create an ideology for a newly modernizing Japan and to suppress the political power of Buddhism. State Shinto, based as it was on flimsy ground, was a "castle in the sand." It vanished the moment the need for the political expediency was gone (Bunce, 1955).

## CHRISTIANITY

Whereas the role of State Shinto can be seen as a reaction against Western power, with disastrous consequences for Japan and the rest of the world, Christianity has played a more direct, albeit minor, role among the Japanese in the modern era. Reischauer and Jansen (1995, p. 212) describe the origins of Christianity in Japan:

> First introduced by the famous Jesuit missionary, Saint Francis Xavier, in 1549, [Christianity] spread more rapidly in Japan during the next several decades than in any other Asian country, and Christians came to number close to half a million. But . . . the early Tokugawa shoguns came to view Christianity as a threat to political unity and suppressed it ruthlessly, creating in the process a large number of Japanese martyrs but virtually stamping the religion out in 1638. Only a few tiny communities of secret Christians survived, and in time they lost most real knowledge of the tenets of their religion.

After the Meiji Restoration of 1868, Christianity became legal and entered Japan freely, brought into the the country by Protestant, Catholic, and other missionaries. At this time, Christians played a major role in the early development of the new education system, and even today, a number of important private secondary schools, colleges, and universities are of Christian origin. However, although Christianity remains intellectually significant (Japanese Christians number among "the best-educated, leading elements in society and have therefore exerted a quite disproportionate influence"), its adherents number less than 2% of the population, divided fairly evenly between Protestants and Catholics (ibid., p. 213). Unlike in Korea, where Christians are now approximately 40% of the population, Christianity has not been able to penetrate modern Japan to any significant degree and its influence remains minor.

## SECULARISM

As Reischauer and Jansen (1995, p. 215) state, "all in all, religion in Japan offers a confused and indistinct picture." One can find Shinto shrines, Buddhist temples, and even the occasional church, everywhere, but in recent times, secularism seems to have become dominant. The cultural anthropologist, Emiko Ohnuki-Tierney, concurs, pointing out that most Japanese people today are extremely secular in outlook, despite leading lives that are intertwined with religious observances (1984, p. 143): "shrine festivals, 'god shelves' and Buddhist altars in the homes, Shinto or Christian marriages, Buddhist funerals, and [Shintoist] rites of passage." Nevertheless, although the majority of Japanese (70–80%) are on some kind of religious roll, "most do not consider themselves believers in any religion" (op. cit.). Some people blame this secularism on the wholesale adoption Western materialism, while others maintain that much of this materialism is generated within Japan itself.

In fact, Ohnuki-Tierney claims that in modern Japan "religious institutions are often intensely commercial. What we see in the visits to temples and shrines is a microcosm of urban Japan [where religion] is wrapped in commercialism, with religious beliefs ranging from deep conviction to almost none (1984, p. 144). She goes on to argue that "there is a wide range of individual beliefs underlying religious institutions in Japan. Some people believe deeply in deities and buddhas . . .; [others] are half-hearted and pay visits to temples and shrines simply because 'it does not hurt anything,' or because the act pleases someone who does believe" (ibid.). She concludes by stating that this "reveals the very secular orientation of the people toward their religions. People ask deities and buddhas for health, prosperity, traffic safety, and various other worldly benefits; they do not focus exclusively on their spiritual well-being or on life after death. It appears that, as they are used by the people, Japanese religions are magical in nature, although they are highly institutionalized" (ibid.).

## NOTES

1. The fleeting world (*ukiyo-e*) was originally a Buddhist concept having to do with the ephemeralness of life, but came to mean "up-to-date" in the Edo period.

2. The emphasis on schooling in Japan stems from the very sources of East Asian civilization. From ancient times, the Chinese stressed the importance of literacy and book learning, and institutionalized these attitudes in a system of scholastic examinations for civil servants (cf. Confucianism). "The Koreans took over this system whole, and the Japanese, though failing to fit it into their [feudal] society, imbibed a deep respect for learning" (Reischauer, 1988, p. 187). In Japan, Buddhist monasteries became centers of learning, and by the late Tokugawa period, much of the education was conducted by private tutoring, although there were also official schools and Confucian academies for samurai. In addition, there were numerous village schools known as *terakoya*, or temple schools, run by Buddhist monks for the children of commoners.

3. According to Reischauer (ibid.), by 1907, all the children were in schools, which was compulsory and free through the six years of coeducational primary school. This was followed by a five-year middle school for boys and girls, then a three-year higher school for boys only, comparable with the German *Gymnasium* or the French *lycée* (vocational schools were also run in parallel). Thereafter, a university could be selected, and the higher schools were entirely in preparation for this post-secondary education.

The whole system was rigorously egalitarian and all students needed to pass entrance examinations, which were designed to be selectors of national leadership. It created a literate mass of soldiers, workers, and housewives with ample technical skills and a thin stream of highly talented young men from the universities who would assume top positions of leadership. These schools were controlled by the government, although a small number of private institutions existed, run by Christian missionaries or Buddhist monks.

4. This vast education effort is in accord with traditional Japanese concepts about the importance of formal education. It is also a natural product of the key role education plays in determining status and function in Japanese society, as there is a close link between academic achievement and success in life. There is little room, however, for self-educated individuals or late bloomers in this system and the great majority of Japan's leaders still come from a small group of prestigious universities (ibid., p. 193).

5. The pre-war Constitution confirmed the privileged position of State Shinto, while guaranteeing freedom of religion. However, this meant that other religious groups were required to receive government approval and that their doctrines and rituals came under official scrutiny.

## DISCUSSION ACTIVITIES

1. Compare and contrast the advantages and disadvantages of education in the Edo period with that in the Meiji era. How were students different in those times than they are today.

2. Some experts say that Japan still suffers from the psychological legacy of *sakoku* (the closed-country policy of the Tokugawa Shogunate), especially in its treatment of foreigners. Do you agree or disagree? Support your arguments with data and facts.

3. At the beginning of the Meiji era, Tokyo University was placed at the top of the educational pyramid in Japan. Do think it is still the best university in the country today? How would you compare the top national universities with the top private ones? What are the advantages and disadvantages of each?

4. Education was clearly a very important factor in the modernization of Japan and in its more recent economic success. Yet the quality of education in the country appears to be declining these days. Do you think this is so? If so, why?

5. It is often claimed that contemporary Japanese society is highly secular and materialistic. Do you agree or disagree? Discuss this issue and its consequences.

6. It is sometimes remarked that Japanese students seem to know very little about the country's history in the late 19th and 20th centuries, particularly the events leading up to World War II. Why do you think this is so? Why is it important for Japanese young people to know their own cultural history?

# APPENDIXES

# APPENDIX A

## ORIGINS OF THE JAPANESE

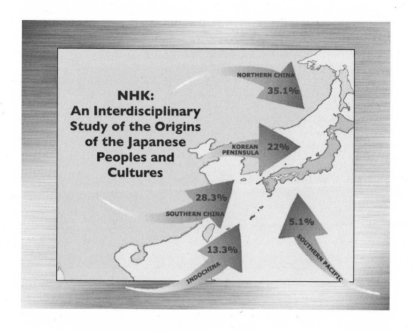

# APPENDIX B

## THE AXIAL AGE

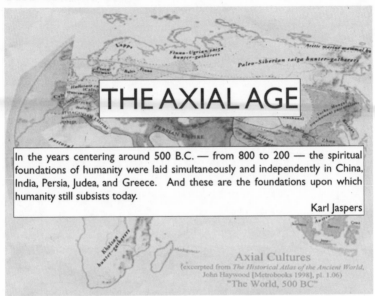

# THE AXIAL AGE

In the years centering around 500 B.C. — from 800 to 200 — the spiritual foundations of humanity were laid simultaneously and independently in China, India, Persia, Judea, and Greece. And these are the foundations upon which humanity still subsists today.

Karl Jaspers

Axial Cultures
(excerpted from *The Historical Atlas of the Ancient World*,
John Haywood [Metrobooks 1998], pl. 1.06)
"The World, 500 BC"

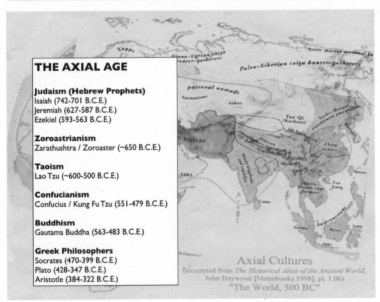

**THE AXIAL AGE**

**Judaism (Hebrew Prophets)**
Isaiah (742-701 B.C.E.)
Jeremiah (627-587 B.C.E.)
Ezekiel (593-563 B.C.E.)

**Zoroastrianism**
Zarathushtra / Zoroaster (~650 B.C.E.)

**Taoism**
Lao Tzu (~600-500 B.C.E.)

**Confucianism**
Confucius / Kung Fu Tzu (551-479 B.C.E.)

**Buddhism**
Gautama Buddha (563-483 B.C.E.)

**Greek Philosophers**
Socrates (470-399 B.C.E.)
Plato (428-347 B.C.E.)
Aristotle (384-322 B.C.E.)

Axial Cultures
(excerpted from *The Historical Atlas of the Ancient World*,
John Haywood [Metrobooks 1998], pl. 1.06)
"The World, 500 BC"

## THE AXIAL AGE
[adapted from Cahill's *Desire of the Everlasting Hills*, 1999, pp. 13–15]

The Axial Age lasted some 300 years—from the late seventh century BC to the late fourth. In Confucian China, it witnessed the development of reasonableness and courtly moderation, as well as the mysticism of the Tao of Lao-Tzu. In India, the Axial Age produced Gautama Buddha, who reformed the chaos of more ancient religious systems and revealed the steps to personal peace. In Iran, the priest Zarathustra taught the Persians the Zoroastrian vision of a cosmic battle between good and evil. To the west, in the tiny kingdoms of Israel and Judah, the Hebrew prophets arose, giving to the monotheism of their people an ethical foundation so profound that it has been the mainstay of the Jewish faith ever since. In the islands and peninsulas of Greece, the Axial Age saw the flowering of what would come to be called "philosophy"—the love of wisdom for its own sake—and of a noble form of politics called "democracy" (*demos* = the people).

All of these ancient civilizations showed distinct similarities to one another—they developed literacy, complex political organizations, elaborate town-planning, advanced metal technologies, and the practice of international diplomacy. During the Axial Age, in all of these cultures, there was a profound tension between political powers and intellectual movements, resulting in attempts everywhere to introduce greater purity, greater justice, greater perfection, and a more universal explanation of things. At this time in the world, new models of reality, either mystical or prophetic or rational, arose as a criticism of, and alternative to, prevailing models.

But these cultural developments proceeded in parallel—they never intersected and never influenced one another except in the most marginal ways. As a result, the world that existed at the beginning of the third century BC was still a world of separate societies, each enclosed by its own characteristic language and values, each with its own Golden Age to look back on, each populated by its own heroes. In the mind of a third-century Athenian, for example, the memory of philosophers such as Socrates and Plato was still strong, and he bore the standards of excellence established by these men within him for reference and judgment. He knew nothing of Abraham and Moses, the figures who lived in the mind of every inhabitant of third-century Jerusalem, just a few miles to the east across the Mediterranean Sea.

As early as the late fourth century BC, this cultural exclusiveness was beginning to dissolve, however. From the western perspective, by the time of Jesus, most of the ancient world—from Asia Minor to the Atlantic, from North Africa to the edges of the vast forests concealing the northern barbarians—had been welded together by forces so strong that, with only a few notable breaks, the cultural unity of the West has held ever since.

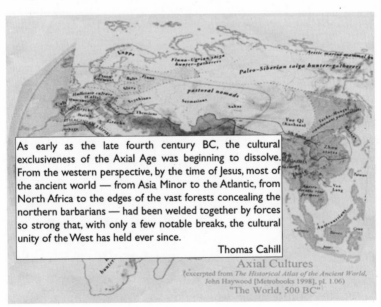

As early as the late fourth century BC, the cultural exclusiveness of the Axial Age was beginning to dissolve. From the western perspective, by the time of Jesus, most of the ancient world — from Asia Minor to the Atlantic, from North Africa to the edges of the vast forests concealing the northern barbarians — had been welded together by forces so strong that, with only a few notable breaks, the cultural unity of the West has held ever since.

Thomas Cahill

Axial Cultures
(excerpted from *The Historical Atlas of the Ancient World*,
John Haywood [Metrobooks 1998], pl. 1.06)
"The World, 500 BC"

# APPENDIX C

## THE MULTILAYERED MODEL OF JAPANESE CULTURE

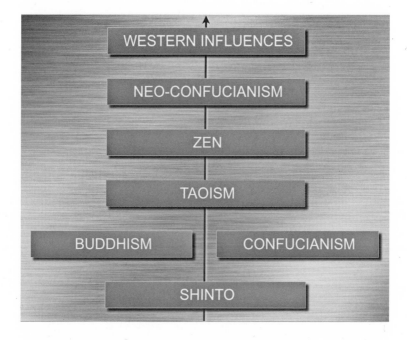

# APPENDIX D

SHOTOKU'S ANALOGY

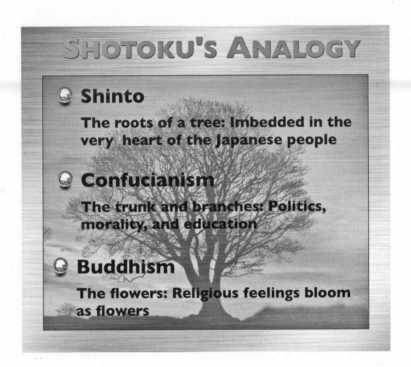

# APPENDIX E

## SHINTO SHRINES ILLUSTRATED

The most outstanding architectural characteristic of Shinto shrines is the simplicity of their construction and ornamentation. Ise Shrine, which is rebuilt in exact replica every twenty years, is considered the purest and most ancient style of Japanese architecture.

Shrines are often surrounded by woods and are places of a serene and solemn atmosphere in which a harmony with nature is sought. Meiji Jingu, for example, is the Shinto shrine dedicated to the souls of Emperor Meiji and his consort, Empress Shoken. After their deaths, people wished to commemorate their virtues and to venerate them, so this shrine was constructed and their souls were enshrined in 1920. Meiji Jingu is covered by an evergreen forest of 120,000 trees of 365 different species, which were donated by people from all parts of Japan. This 700,000 square-meter forest is visited by many people, both as a spiritual home of the people and as a recreation and relaxation area in the center of Tokyo.

One or more gates (*torii*) mark the approach and entrance to a Shinto shrine. They come in various colors, most are made of wood, and many are painted orange and black. The *torii* separate the sacred space of the shrine from the outside world.

## TORII

## SHITO SHRINE

The *torii* marking the entrance to shrines can be seen throughout the countryside in Japan, like at Kijigoto Shrine in Fukuoka.

KIJIGOTO SHRINE

*Torii* can even be seen in the sea in coastal areas around Japan, as with the famous Futamigaura Shrine in Mie Prefecture.

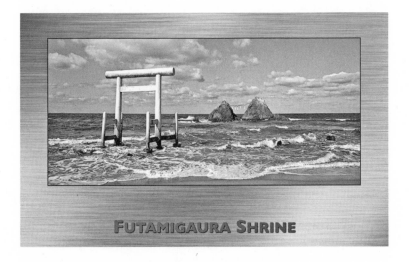

FUTAMIGAURA SHRINE

Japanese cities are also the homes of many shrines. Izumo Shrine below is a typical example.

IZUMO SHRINE

The gates marking the entrance to shrines are usually draped with a *shimenawa*, a straw festoon with paper streamers that hang from it. *Shimenawa* are frequently used in Japan to mark sacred spaces or objects and also hang directly over spots where people make offerings and pray to the deity of the shrine. (A rope similar to the *shimenawa* is

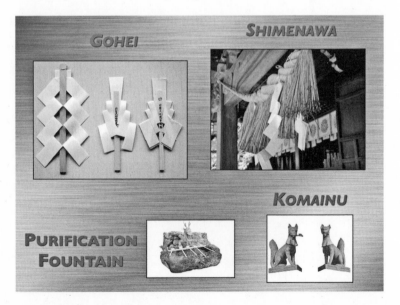

GOHEI

SHIMENAWA

PURIFICATION FOUNTAIN

KOMAINU

also worn by *yokozuna*, the highest ranked sumo wrestlers, during ritual ceremonies.)

On each side of a shrine's entrance, there are often statues of a pair of guardian dogs, called *komainu*.

In most shrines, a purification fountain can be found at the entrance. The water from these fountains is used for purification, as people clean their hands and mouths before approaching the main hall.

Depending on a shrine's architectural style, the main hall (*honden*) and offering hall (*haiden*) are two seperate buildings or combined into one building. The main hall's innermost chamber contains the shrine's sacred objects, while visitors make prayers and offerings at the offering hall. In addition, stages for *bugaku* dance or *noh* theater performances can be found at some shrines.

Many shrine visitors write their wishes on wooden plates, called *ema*, and then leave them at the shrine in the hope that their wishes come true. Most people wish for good health, success in business, passing entrance exams, love or wealth, and so forth. *Omikuji*, or fortune telling paper slips, are also found at many shrines. Randomly drawn, they contain predictions ranging from *daikichi* ("great good luck") to *daikyo* ("great bad luck"). By tying the piece of paper around a tree's branch, good fortune will come true or bad fortune can be averted.

Within the shrines, there is no provision made for a congregation, and only the space for an altar and priests and attendants is needed. Individual worshippers stand outside to make their petition, and worship consists of obeisance, offerings, prayers, and the clapping of hands to attract the attention of the *kami*. Over time, a symbolic offering came into use in which strips of paper representing the strips of cloth were attached to a wand (*gohei*) and placed on the altar. It was thought that *kami* descended into these wands, and *gohei* became objects of worship themselves.

# APPENDIX F

## THE SPREAD OF BUDDHISM

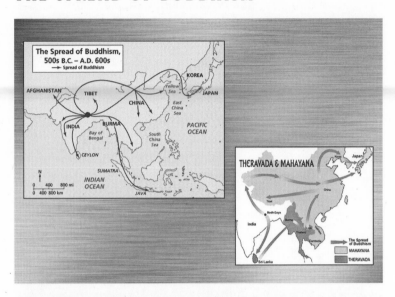

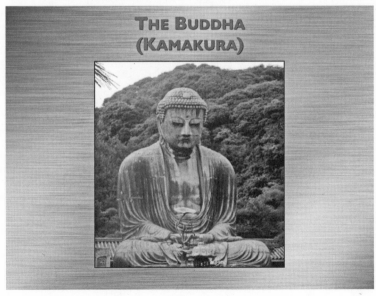

# APPENDIX G

## YIN/YANG AND THE 64 HEXAGRAMS

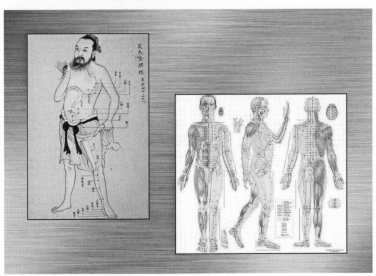

Acupuncture

# APPENDIX H

## ZEN SCHOOLS

# APPENDIX I

## JAPANESE AESTHETICS

Aesthetics is of primary importance in virtually all forms of cultural expression in Japan. Keene (1988, p. 3) states that "the Japanese sense of beauty [is] perhaps the central element in all of Japanese culture," while Kishimoto (as cited in Moore, 1967, p. 296) speaks of the aesthetic as "being so significant as to be identical with the religious in Japan." In fact, Moore (ibid.) argues that aesthetics is "the outstanding positive characteristic of Japanese culture as a whole—as of the very essence of Japanese life." It has been considered the "essentially unique expression of spirituality in Japan," akin to ethics in China, religion in India, and reason and logic in the West (ibid.).

Aesthetics, which has played such a prominent role in the cultural life of Japan since ancient times, has its roots in the two major religions of the country—Shinto and Buddhism. Shinto's influence can be felt mainly in a continuing reverence for both nature and purity, and from Buddhism comes all of the most basic Japanese attitudes toward aesthetics. Zen is the strain of Buddhism to have most thoroughly pervaded artistry in Japanese life. It produced a "tremendous cross-fertilization of philosophical, scholarly, poetic, and artistic pursuits in which the Zen and Taoist feeling for 'naturalness' became the dominant note" (Watts, 1957, p. 177). As in China, Japanese Zen monasteries became leading centers of scholarship [in which] "the roles of scholar, artist, and poet were not widely separated" (ibid.). Zen monks created works of art as formalizations of a way of life (unlike members of other Buddhist sects who developed art mainly for worship or prayer), and the universal appeal of such art forms as paintings, calligraphy, and tea ceremony led to their transformation from formalized aspects of ancient monastic life to forms of contemporary Japanese art (Mizuo, 1970, p. 161).

A number of key elements in the Japanese sense of aesthetics have been identified by Keene (1988) in an examination of the classic work *Tsurezuregusa* (*Essays in Idleness*), written in the 14th century by the Buddhist monk Kenko. Although unknown to the reading public in his lifetime, Kenko's work came to prominence in the 17th century, and according to Keene (1988, p. 5), not only reflected the tastes of the Japanese of much earlier times, but also "greatly contributed to the formation of the aesthetic preferences of Japanese for centuries to come."

On the basis of Kenko's work, Keene suggests that four characteristics are of special importance in understanding Japanese aesthetic values: (1) suggestion, (2) irregularity, (3) simplicity, and (4) perishability (impermanence).

## SUGGESTION

The use of suggestion as an aesthetic principle is described in the following passage from *Essays in Idleness*:

> Are we to look at cherry blossoms only in full bloom, the moon only when it is cloudless? To long for the moon while looking on the rain, to lower the blinds and be unaware of the passing of spring—these are even more deeply moving. (as cited in Fister-Stoga, 1993, p. 142)

This feeling of the beauty of suggestion seems in direct contrast to the Western ideal which tends to place more value on climactic moments such as a rose in full bloom or when the soprano hits "high C." The principle of suggestion is also conveyed in innumerable Japanese love poems which almost never express the joy of actually meeting the beloved, but instead describe the poet's yearning for such a meeting, or else the sad realization that an affair is over. This seems to reflect a Japanese preference for beginnings and endings rather than moments of fulfillment (Keene, 1988, p. 9). In Japanese ink paintings, as well, the desire to suggest rather than state in full can be readily found—a few brush strokes serve to suggest ranges of mountains, a single stroke a stalk of bamboo. As Keene (ibid.) notes, "a mountain painted in green can never be any color but green, but a mountain whose outlines are given with a few brush strokes of black ink can be any color."

## IRREGULARITY

The principle of irregularity in Japanese aesthetic expression can be found in a number of different forms: the incomplete, the imperfect, and the asymmetrical. As Kenko states: "In everything, no matter what it may be, uniformity is undesirable. Leaving something incomplete makes it interesting, and gives one the feeling that there is room for growth." Another priest, Abbot Koyu, adds: "It is typical of the unintelligent man to insist on assembling complete sets of everything. Imperfect sets are better" (as cited in Keene, 1988, p. 10). In this preference for imperfect forms can be seen the Japanese idea that beauty is "never something that has been brought to completion" (Itoh; as cited in Claiborne, 1993, p. 73). "The Japanese have long been partial not only to incompleteness but also to another variety of irregularity, asymmetry" (Keene, 1988, p. 10), and in this respect, they differ from other peoples of Asia. In Chinese art and architecture one finds symmetry: what is on the right side is likely to be a mirror image of what is on the left. The typical layout of a Chinese monastery, for example, has the same buildings on one side of a central axis as on the other. But in Japan, even though the original plans were imported from China, buildings seem to cluster on one side or the other. In poems too, irregular numbers of lines are found—five for *tanka* and three for haiku—in contrast to the quatrains typical of the poetic forms of most of the rest of the world. This same tendency is found in calligraphy: "Japanese children are taught in calligraphy lessons never to bisect a horizontal stroke with a vertical one: the vertical stroke should always cross the horizontal one at some point not equidistant from both ends. A symmetrical character is considered to be 'dead'" (ibid.). The calligraphic style most respected by the Japanese tends to be highly individual; copybook perfection is not admired. Irregularity is also a feature of Japanese ceramics—the most admired wares are never regular in shape and even glaze is applied in such a way as to leave occasional bald patches. Nor do flower arrangements and gardens in Japan emphasize Western-style geometrical precision. The symmetry of the gardens at Versailles, for example, is in marked contrast to the asymmetry of the rock garden of the Ryōanji with its fifteen randomly placed stones.

## SIMPLICITY

Kenko writes in another passage from *Essays in Idleness*: "It is excellent for a man to be simple in his tastes, to avoid extravagance, to own no possessions, to entertain no craving for worldly success" (as cited in Keene, 1988, p. 14). This quotation clearly reflects certain Buddhist beliefs, but also the long-held Japanese admiration for simplicity. It is felt that traditional Japanese homes at their most artistic, for example, should have plenty of spare room and too little rather than too much furniture, illustrating the "less is more" preference for simplicity. The avoidance of displays of conspicuous wealth in furnishing a home is also typical of the Japanese insistence on simplicity—the Japanese preference for high quality, unpainted wood is now much admired throughout the world. Simplicity as an aesthetic principle is not confined just to houses and furnishings. Perhaps the most striking example of the Japanese love for unobtrusive elegance is the tea ceremony. The great teamaster, Rikyu, is said to have sought the ideal of *sabi* (or rust)—"a preference for a rusty-looking kettle to one of gleaming newness" (ibid., p. 16). A further example of the value of simplicity in Japan can be found in food. "Japanese cuisine lacks the intensity of flavor of foods found in other countries in Asia. Spices are seldom used; garlic almost never" (ibid., p. 17). The taste of natural ingredients, untampered by sauces, is the ideal of Japanese cuisine. Just as the faint perfume of the plum blossom is preferred to the heavy odor of the lily, subtle and barely perceptible differences in flavor are prized in Japan (ibid.).

## PERISHABILITY (IMPERMANENCE)

In Japan, perishability rather than permanence has long
been an aesthetic ideal, as Hearn (as cited in Keene, 1988,
p. 18) contends: "Generally speaking [in the West] we construct for endurance, the Japanese for impermanency. Few
things for common use are made in Japan with a view to
durability." A passage from *Essays in Idleness* illustrates this
traditional national preference for the impermanent: "It is
only after the silk wrapper has frayed at top and bottom,
and the mother-of-pearl has fallen from the roller that a
scroll looks beautiful" (ibid.). In other words, signs of wear
and tear are sometimes considered a sign of good taste; in
works of art, flaws are often as attractive as intrinsic beauty.
The frailty and perishability of human existence is also a
common theme in Japanese literature and is almost a necessary condition of beauty. Thus, Kenko wrote:

> If a man were never to fade away like the dews of Adash-
> ino, never to vanish like the smoke over Toribeyama, but
> lingered on forever in this world, how things would lose
> their power over us! The most precious thing in life is its
> uncertainty. (ibid., p. 20)

The special love of the Japanese for cherry blossoms, as
well, is surely connected with the appreciation of perishability. Cherry blossoms, after all, normally fall after three
brief days of flowering, "a fact that countless poets have had
occasion to lament" (ibid., p. 21).

## CONCLUSION

As Keene (ibid., p. 22) notes, however, visitors who expect to find exquisite beauty everywhere in Japan today are likely to be shocked in their first encounters with contemporary Japanese culture: vending machines on every corner, the ugliness of commercial signs, the concrete playgrounds, the lack of parks and other green living spaces, the ubiquitous fast-food shops of every kind. In matters of taste, the Japanese seem, as in so many other areas, paradoxical in nature. Some would say that there are no people who are more sensitive to beauty than the Japanese; others point out that a more convenient life is often more important than any sense of beauty or tradition in Japan. Nevertheless, the aesthetic sentiments of the Japanese people, which have been shaped by many centuries of predominantly Shinto and Buddhist influence, are still strong in modern Japan, and often find surprising outlets for expression.

# APPENDIX J

## Confucius

# AFTERWORD

Since this book evolved out of a specific approach to teaching Japanese cultural history at a number of universities in Japan, it is perhaps appropriate to conclude with some comments on the state of history teaching in our schools in general today. It is said that a knowledge of history brings perspective and proportion; yet perspective and proportion are all too often missing in the current debate on how history should be taught in our education systems. History has always been a controversial and contentious subject, but these days, it is often so "politically toxic" that no one seems to want to touch it. At best, in most schools, it usually involves the rote memorization of disconnected dates, figures, and events for regurgitation on state-sponsored examinations, leaving little scope for the kind of overarching perspective needed to provide an adequate understanding among learners.

In contrast, the approach used in this book is based on the development of a conceptual framework, the multilayered model, which provides the infrastructure necessary for a broad understanding of Japanese cultural history. It is important to note here that a model is an abstract representation of reality. The two key words in this definition are *abstract* and *representation*. A model is not supposed to be exactly like reality. Rather, it *represents* the real world by *abstracting*, or taking from it, that which will help us understand it. There is much in the real world that a model must leave out. When building a model, how can one know which details to include and which to leave aside? There is no simple answer to this question. The right amount of detail depends on one's purpose in building the model in the first place, but in most cases, keeping a model simple makes it easier to see basic, underlying principles at work.

In the case of the multilayered model used in *Japanese Culture: The Religious and Philosophical Foundations*, the descriptions of each layer, taken separately, necessarily leave much out. Yet, when combined into a cohesive whole, this conceptual framework provides an overview of Japanese cultural history that is simple, elegant, and easy to understand. It is hoped that this clarity and scope of vision will provide readers with a useful starting point for their own further explorations of this complex and fascinating culture.

# BIBLIOGRAPHY

Arakawa, K., & Davies, R. (2001). *Nihonjin no kokoro: The Japanese sense of self. Ehime University Center for Educational Research and Practice Memoirs, 19*, 71–86.

Armstrong, K. (1993). *A history of God: The 4000-year quest of Judaism, Christianity and Islam.* New York: Ballentine Books.

Barnlund, D. (1989). *Public and private self in Japan and the United States: Communicative styles of two cultures.* Yarmouth, MN: Intercultural Press.

Benedict, R. (1946). *The chrysanthemum and the sword.* Tokyo: Tuttle.

Bix, H. (2000). *Hirohito and the making of modern Japan.* New York: Harper Collins.

Breen, J. (2000). *Shinto in history.* New York: Routledge.

Breen, J., & Teeuwen, M. (Eds.). (2000). *Shinto in history: Ways of the kami.* Honolulu: University of Hawai'i Press.

Bunce, W. (1955). *Religions in Japan: Buddhism, Shinto, Christianity.* Rutland, VT: Tuttle.

Cahill, T. (1995). *How the Irish saved civilization: The untold story of Ireland's heroic role from the fall of Rome to the rise of medieval Europe.* New York: Anchor Books.

Cahill, T. (1998). *The gifts of the Jews: How a tribe of desert nomads changed the way everyone thinks and feels.* New York: Anchor Books.

Cahill, T. (1999). *Desire of the everlasting hills: The world before and after Jesus.* New York: Anchor Books.

Campbell, J. (1959). *The masks of God: Primitive mythology.* New York: Penguin Arkana Series.

Campbell, J. (1962). *The masks of God: Oriental mythology.* New York: Penguin Arkana Series.

Campbell, J. (1964). *The masks of God: Occidental mythology.* New York: Penguin Arkana Series.

Campbell, J. (1968). *The masks of God: Creative mythology*. New York: Penguin Arkana Series.

Claiborne, G. (1993). *Japanese and American rhetoric: A contrastive study*. Unpublished doctoral dissertation. University of South Florida.

Cohen, W. (2000). *East Asia at the center: Four thousand years of engagement with the world*. New York: Columbia University Press.

Davies, R., & Ikeno, O. (Eds.). (2002). *The Japanese mind: Understanding contemporary Japanese culture*. Tokyo: Tuttle.

De Bary, W. (1988). *East Asian civilizations: A dialogue in five stages*. Cambridge, MA: Harvard University Press.

Doi, T. (1973). *The anatomy of dependence [Amae no kouzou]*. Tokyo: Kodansha International.

Doi, T. (1985). *The anatomy of self: The individual versus society [Omote to ura]*. Tokyo: Kodansha International.

Dower, J. (1999). *Embracing defeat. Japan in the wake of World War II*. New York: W.W. Norton.

Drury, N. (1989). *The elements of shamanism*. Shaftesbury, Dorset: Element Books.

Efron, S. (1996, December 17). Cleaning up on hygiene mania. *The Daily Yomiuri*, p. 9.

Eggington, W. (1987). Written academic discourse in Korean: Implications for effective communication. In U. Connor & R. Kaplan (Eds.), *Writing across languages: Analysis of L2 text*. Reading, MA: Addison-Wesley.

Enkvist, N. (1987). Text linguistics for the applier: An orientation. In U. Connor & R. Kaplan (Eds.), *Writing across languages: Analysis of L2 Text* (pp. 23–44). Reading, MA: Addison-Wesley.

Finkelstein, B., Imamura, A., & Tobin, J. (Eds.). (1991). *Transcending stereotypes: Discovering Japanese culture and education*. Yarmouth, MN: Intercultural Press.

Fister-Stoga, F. (1993). Convention and composition in the Japanese ki-sho-ten-ketsu: Towards a methodology of contrastive rhetoric. *Gaikokugoka Kenkyukyo* [Proceedings of the Department of Foreign Languages and Literature College of Arts and Sciences, University of Tokyo] *XLI*(3), 130–168.

Garon, S. (1997). *Molding Japanese minds: The state in everyday life*. Princeton: Princeton University Press.

Gluck, C. (1985). *Japan's modern myths: Ideology in the late Meiji period*. Princeton: Princeton University Press.

Gordenker, A. (2003, June 6). National hygiene begins in the classroom. *The Japan Times*, p. 17.

Grigg, R. (1994). *The tao of Zen*. Tokyo: Tuttle.

Hall, J. (1971). *Japan from prehistory to modern times*. Tokyo: Tuttle.

Hall, I. (1998). *Cartels of the mind: Japan's intellectual closed shop*. New York: W.W. Norton.

Hall, J., & Beardsley, R. (1965). *Twelve doors to Japan*. New York: McGraw-Hill.

Hanley, S. (1997). *Everyday things in premodern Japan*. Berkeley: University of California Press.

Hearn, L. (1904). *Japan: An attempt at interpretation*. New York: Macmillan.

Hinds, J. (1983). Contrastive rhetoric: Japanese and English. *Text*, 3(2), 183–195.

Hoffman, M. (2006, September 10). Confucius and his golden age. *The Japan Times*, p. 7.

Hori, I. (1967). The appearance of individual self-consciousness in Japanese religion and its historical transformations. In C. Moore (Ed.), *The Japanese mind* (pp. 201–227). Rutland, VT: Tuttle.

Keegan, J. (1994). *A history of warfare*. New York: Vintage Books.

Keene, D. (1988). *The pleasures of Japanese literature*. New York: Columbia University Press.

Kerr, A. (1996). *Lost Japan*. Singapore: Lonely Planet Publications.

Kisala, R. (1999). *Prophets of peace: Pacifism and cultural identity in Japan's new religions.* Honolulu: University of Hawai'i Press.

*Kodansha encyclopedia of Japan* (Vol. 8). (1983). Tokyo: Kodansha.

Kodansha International. (1996). *Keys to the Japanese heart and soul.* Tokyo: Author.

Kumeta, N. (1997, January 11). Japan hard on disabled [Letter to the Editor]. *The Daily Yomiuri*, p. 6.

LaPenta, J. (1998, May 10). A classic look at Edo 'chic'. *The Daily Yomiuri*, p. 15.

Lebra, T. Sugiyama. (1976). *Japanese patterns of behavior.* Honolulu: The University Press of Hawai'i.

Lebra, T. Sugiyama, & Lebra, W. (Eds.). (1974). *Japanese culture and behavior.* Honolulu: The University Press of Hawai'i.

Mann, A. T. (1995). *The elements of reincarnation.* Shaftesbury, Dorset: Element Books.

Matsui, Y. (1996). *Women in the new Asia.* London: Zen Books.

McConnell, D. (2000). *Importing diversity: Inside Japan's JET program.* Berkeley: University of California Press.

McCormack, G. (1996). *The emptiness of Japanese affluence.* New York: M.E. Sharpe.

McVeigh, B. (2002). *Japanese higher education as myth.* New York. M.E. Sharpe.

Miller, R. (1982). *Japan's modern myth: The language and beyond.* Tokyo: Weatherhill.

Miyamoto, M. (1993). *Straitjacket society: An insider's irreverent view of bureaucratic Japan.* Tokyo: Kodasha International.

Mizuo, H. (1970). Zen art. *Japan Quarterly*, 17, 160–166.

Moore, C. (1967). *The Japanese mind: Essentials of Japanese philosophy and culture.* Tokyo: Tuttle.

Munsterberg, H. (1965). *Zen and oriental art.* Tokyo: Tuttle.

Nakamura, H. (1971). *Ways of thinking of eastern peoples: India-China-Tibet-Japan.* Honolulu: University of Hawaii Press.

Nakane, C. (1970). *Japanese society.* Tokyo: Tuttle.

Oe, K. (1994). *Japan, the ambiguous, and myself: The Nobel Prize speech and other lectures.* Tokyo: Kodansha International.

Ohnuki-Tierney, E. (1984). *Illness and culture in contemporary Japan.* Cambridge: Cambridge University Press.

Ohnuki-Tierney, E. (1987). *The monkey as mirror: Symbolic transformations in Japanese history and ritual.* Princeton: Princeton University Press.

Ohnuki-Tierney, E. (1993). *Rice as self: Japanese identities through time.* Princeton: Princeton University Press.

Okano, K., & Tsuchiya, M. (1999). *Education in contemporary Japan: Inequity and diversity.* Cambridge: Cambridge University Press.

Ono, J. (1995, January 13). Hospitals shun HIV-positive patients. *The Daily Yomiuri,* p. 12.

Palmer, M. (1991). *The elements of Taoism.* Shaftesbury, Dorset: Element Books.

Porter, M., Takeuchi, H., & Sakakibara, M. (2000). *Can Japan compete?* London: Macmillan.

Pyle, K. (2007). *Japan rising: The resurgence of Japanese power and purpose.* New York: Public Affairs Books.

Reischauer, E. (1988). *The Japanese today.* Cambridge, MA: Belknap Press.

Reischauer, E., & Jansen, M. (1995). *The Japanese today: Change and continuity.* Cambridge, MA: Harvard University Press.

Richie, D. (1997). *Partial views: Essays on contemporary Japan.* Tokyo: The Japan Times.

Rolling back democracy. *The Japan Times,* May 31, 2000, p. 20.

Sakamaki, S. (1967). Shinto: Japanese ethnocentrism. In C. Moore (Ed.), *The Japanese mind* (pp. 24–32). Rutland, VT: Tuttle.

Sansom, G. (1931/1976). *Japan—A short cultural history* (Vols. 1–3). Tokyo: Tuttle.

Sasamoto, H. (1999, January 26). One man's quest for Japanese identity. *The Daily Yomiuri,* p. 7.

Schnell, S. (1999). *The rousing drum: Ritual practice in a Japanese community.* Honolulu: University of Hawai'i Press.

Scott, D., & Doubleday, T. (1992). *The elements of Zen*. Shaftesbury, Dorset: Element Books.

Simpkins, A., & Simpkins, C. (1997). *Zen around the world: A 2500-year journey from the Buddha to you*. Tokyo: Tuttle.

Simpkins, A., & Simpkins, C. (1999). *Simple Taoism: A guide to living in balance*. Tokyo: Tuttle.

Simpkins, A., & Simpkins, C. (1999). *Simple Zen: A guide to living moment by moment*. Tokyo: Tuttle.

Smith, P. (1997). *Japan: A reinterpretation*. New York: Pantheon Books.

Smith, H. (1991). *The world's religions: Our great wisdom traditions*. New York: HarperCollins.

Smith, R. (1974). *Ancestor worship in contemporary Japan*. Stanford, CA: Stanford University Press.

Snelling, J. (1990). *The elements of Buddhism*. Shaftesbury, Dorset: Element Books.

Suzuki, D. (1959). *Zen and Japanese culture*. Princeton: Princeton University Press.

Suzuki, D. (1964). *An introduction to Zen Buddhism*. New York: Evergreen Black Cat-Grove.

Tarnas, R. (1991). *The passion of the western mind: Understanding the ideas that have shaped our world view*. New York: Ballentine.

Thought control uncovered: Document shows pressure on scholars (2006, December 17). *The Japan Times*, p. 27.

Tsuru, S. (1993). *Japan's capitalism: Creative defeat and beyond*. Cambridge: Cambridge University Press.

Watts, A. (1957). *The way of Zen*. New York: Pantheon.

Watts, A. (1995). *The philosophies of Asia*. Tokyo: Tuttle.

Watts, A. (1996). *Buddhism: The religion of no-religion*. Tokyo: Tuttle.

Watts, A. (1997). *Taoism: Way beyond seeing*. Tokyo: Tuttle.

Yato, T. (1996, December 18). World of Japanese judo gets thrown for a loop. *The Daily Yomiuri*, p. 7.